In Sickness and In Health

Lessons Learned on the Journey from Cystic Fibrosis to Total Health

Mandy B. Anderson

D1738237

In Sickness and In Health

Printed in the United States of America
ISBN-13: 978-0615541105
ISBN-10: 0615541100

DEDICATION

God Almighty, my Jehovah Rapha, may you have your way with this book!

To Nate, my Constant Encourager, Protector, Love of my life, and Best Friend. May God continue to raise you up to be a light on a hill for all to see!

To every Human Soul who has a desire for better health, true wholeness, and healing - may this book give you the life skills needed to start your journey. Thank you for your dedication to living beyond your circumstances!

ACKNOWLEDGEMENTS

The One True God - Thank you for allowing me to walk this beautiful journey of sickness to total health, and for moving heaven and earth so I could live my life in true wholeness of who you designed me to be. Thank you for taking my sickness upon yourself so that I may have life in abundance, and for making my days many while adding years to my life. I am nothing without you, and my life is yours.

Nate - Thank you for partnering with me in this beautiful, crazy life! You have spoken health over me since I met you, and for that you are my hero! Your encouragement to write this book and share this story has been the thing that kept me going when the task seemed overwhelming. Thank you for supporting my dreams, and for walking the journey with me. I love you more than words can express and I am so honored to be your wife!

Mom and Dad - Your years of sacrifice and diligence so that I could have a healthy, normal life were not in vain. Thank you for keeping me healthy, for teaching me to always take care of myself, and for encouraging me to go after my dreams. Most of all, thank you for teaching me to have faith in Jesus Christ! I love you both so much and am honored to have you as my parents!

Joy Randall - Thank you so much for your work on this project. Your expertise, guidance, and friendship made this process a breeze. Thank you for your prayers and the words of life that you spoke over my dreams and specifically this book. You are an amazing, talented woman and it has been an honor to work with you!

Thea Woods - Girl, you are amazing! Your work on the cover of this book was such a blessing to me. Keep it up because there are amazing things in your future!

Dani Johnson - I will be forever grateful that you picked up your mat and walked! Thank you for being my coach and mentor and for speaking life over these once dead bones.

Sandi Krakowski - Your insight and coaching has made me a better writer and a stronger warrior in the battle against sickness. Thank you from the bottom of my heart!

LaVonne Atnip - Thank you for your prayers and for reminding me about the power of my very own tongue. Your tip about speaking God's word over my own body has become my secret weapon!

My Beloved Family, Friends, & Health Professionals - Each of you has touched my heart deeply. Thank you for your prayers and encouragement over the years. I would not be who I am today without the imprint you have left on my heart. May

God bless each of you abundantly with health and may all go well with you!

My JP+ Team - Thank you so much for your encouragement over the years. I am so honored to work with such an amazing group of people with a heart for total health!

You, my client and friend - Thank you for picking up this book. Your desire for better health and true wholeness was put there from the moment that you were knit together in your mother's womb. There is a story sprouting inside of you, and this is just the beginning of living beyond your circumstances. I can't wait to hear how this book impacts you so that your story can be shared!

TESTIMONIALS

"In Sickness and In Health is a book that is Spiritually Uplifting! Not only does it encourage self-reflection but, makes you want to grasp every ounce of life you are given. It's a beautiful story full of LIFE! A real example of conquering and overcoming wars within one's self! It is a book I will continuously reference. I found a truth in everything you spoke of and I know others will also!!! It's comforting to know that I'm not alone in the outlook of this Crazy Beautiful Life God has Granted us with!"

~ Sarah Volner

"People's lives are going to be changed by this book. It was thought provoking, hard-hitting, and honest. This is a book that people will be coming back to again and again to re-read, underline, and learn from. "In Sickness and In Health" brought me to tears, challenged my assumptions, and caused me to think twice about some things I was doing in my life."

~ Raychel Chumley, Life & Marriage Coach

www.daybreakcoachingservices.com

"This book is an easy read that makes the individual dig a little deeper inside of themselves. I had a hard time putting it down!"

~ Tara Caudle PT, DPT

"What a wonderful book! It really helped me to examine my own excuses and why I can't overcome fear. If you feel alone, depressed, or unfulfilled then read this book. It will challenge you to make for yourself a better life. Thank you Mandy!"

~ Lance M.

"In Sickness and In Health is a book for everybody, not just those living with Cystic Fibrosis or another disease. Nurses are taught to give holistic care to their patients, so as an RN, I really appreciate that Mandy talks about the importance of taking care of our whole self. I know that in order to have total wellness we need to work on more than just our physical health. This book is encouraging, inspirational, and emotional. Mandy gives us easy steps to help us rise above whatever our situation may be to live the life we all deserve... a life of true wholeness and hope."

~ Jandi Theis, RN, Wellness Educator

www.EverydayEncouragement.com

"The journey of life encompasses many aspects of physical, psycho-social, biochemical and spiritual stresses, whether good or bad! Your individual perception is the key to your success, happiness and health. Motivation is an outside in phenomenon, whereas inspiration is an inside out phenomenon. You, yes you, had the choice to be the best you ever when you woke this morning! Did you ask yourself, while facing the mirror this morning...Will I reflect the world or will the world reflect me? Think long and hard about that question. Your thoughts create your feelings, choose the good ones!

As a Doctor of Chiropractic I am privileged to watch the innate intelligence express itself in terms of health daily. I often am asked by patients, how long do you think I will need care. My response, are you open to a different approach, are you willing to understand health is a journey and without a positive mindset your body will never be able to express itself, 100%.

It is not to my amazement that I am contributing to this book. What is amazing is that so many people give up on themselves. Mrs. Anderson was one who knew her purpose, found a wellness team and continues to strive towards overall core health and well-being! I am honored and blessed to have such a person as Mrs. Anderson in my life. I hope this book awakens your awareness of the powerful life force within us all!"

~ Dr. Dustin J. Barton, Core Health Chiro

"This book was a breath of fresh air. Not only are the tips and goals easy to understand, but they made me feel like I can follow through with them. The things I have learned and used in my own life from this book have changed my health and my marriage in the first few weeks. Thank you, Mandy, for your words of life!"

~ Madison Moericke

CONTENTS

THIS JOURNEY

Every day we make decisions. Some are small, and some are quite large.

Today you made a decision about what time to wake up and whether or not you jumped out of bed or pushed the snooze button. Then, you chose what to wear and how to do your hair. If you are the type of person who does everything you can to stay healthy, you had a nutritious breakfast and faithfully took all of your supplements.

Maybe you decided to stop at Starbucks on the way to work because that's your one guilty pleasure. Or maybe your breakfast came entirely from Starbucks—Venti Caramel Machiatto with extra whip cream and a scrumptious muffin or oatmeal. Maybe you skipped breakfast all together, because that's just how you roll. Either way, you made some pretty important decisions, long before you punched the time clock.

How about this…what did you decide to think about on your way to work? Chances are your mind was filled with thoughts about your day, how you looked, what others might think, what others might say…maybe you even pondered words that were spoken over you yesterday that ticked you off or hurt your feelings. You may have had thoughts of how you were going to pay your rent, feed your children, get out of debt, or even how you were ever going to reach the dream life that floats around in the back of your mind. Or maybe you dwelled on the report that the doctor gave you when he called right before you ran out the door.

You made hundreds of decisions before you decided to pick up this book and start reading it. And here you are, wondering what the point is.

The point is, most of us don't pay attention to the choices we make or how they shape our world. When it comes to our health and the quality of our lives, we tend to see it as the "luck of the draw" we have no control over. Have you ever met someone who woke up one day and decided they were going to have cancer; or someone who decides to go into debt, on purpose, and is proud to tell you about it? We don't make these decisions consciously, but many times our choices direct our path.

Obviously we don't have control over all our circumstances. Those born with life-threatening diseases didn't have control over that. Victims of natural disasters didn't have control over what happened either. But there is one truth that often gets swept under the table or hidden altogether no matter what our circumstances.

That truth is this: **We always have a choice**; we can choose to live our lives in true wholeness and health, or we can choose to give up and give in.

When it comes to our health and quality of life, we always have a choice. For instance, you can decide right now how you handle your health, and you can decide to change your health to the best of your ability from this point forward. Mark my words—you do not have to accept a life of sickness! Just because sickness of any kind might be in your family history, or you were born with a life-threatening disease that daily threatens your well-being; those circumstances do not determine the course of your life!

You always have a choice.

Where does my passion about this subject come from? It comes from a lifetime of yearning to inspire others to overcome their circumstances based on my lifetime of overcoming the odds.

I was born with a disease called Cystic Fibrosis, a genetic disease that affects the respiratory and digestive systems. Basically, in a nutshell, your body makes really thick mucus, and lots of it, so you can barely breathe and you can't digest food because your body's natural enzymes get stuck in the mucus and can't do their job. Sounds kind of gross, huh? To ease your mind, remember this: every human body makes mucus. With Cystic Fibrosis (CF, as it will be referred to from here on) it's just an extra special mucus. *wink*

At six months old, I was diagnosed. My parents had been concerned because I was constantly sick with colds and bronchitis and wasn't gaining any weight—even though I was eating constantly. So, it turns out that was because of CF. Thus started a change in lifestyle that included breathing treatments twice a day and a continuous intake of enzymes in the form of horse pills to digest food and gain weight. I've been a pill popper since I was a baby!

At the time of my diagnosis, my parents were told not to expect me to live past the age of a grade school student and to graduate from high school was a low probability, which if I did would certainly be considered a miracle. That was the reality of life with CF back in 1981. Well, this is the story of one of many living miracles because I did graduate from high school and medical technology and holistic approaches have come a long way since then.

I remember sitting in church the day of my high school graduation—it was a small church. My parents stood up and began to thank everyone for their support over the years. Then they shared how that day was so special to them because they never dreamed it would come. They basically shared my whole life story in twenty minutes, including some of the not so fun details of what living with CF can be like, while I sat there red-faced with embarrassment!

Why was I so embarrassed? Ok, think back to being a teenager for a moment; would you have been thrilled to have your parents cry publicly as they talked about you and shared your life story? The last thing most teenagers want is for their parents to get up and make a spectacle of themselves in public, let alone cry when they do it! So yes, I was the embarrassed teenager who hadn't matured enough to see and appreciate the miracle they were experiencing.

That wasn't the only miracle. Many miracles have happened since my diagnosis. The most obvious include living long enough to get married and being able to run a 5K in thirty seven minutes with no pain, no gasping or fighting for air or, for that matter, for my life. My quality of life is thriving and vibrant! Even though it's miraculous and exciting, it's a very emotional story to share, because it hasn't been an easy road to walk.

When I got married and started living my life as an adult and not a child, I entered a dark season and began to hide behind CF. Growing up a very positive person, I'm not sure why I fell into such a pit, but I did. CF became a crutch I used. Like one winter when I was battling with my health, I got my doctor to give me a note stating that I needed a parking spot closer to the door because the cold air would burn my lungs. As you can see from my request, exercise wasn't a part of my routine at that time so my lungs were very sensitive. A parking pass was given; the crutch worked. I used things like that to my advantage—a lot...and all it did was keep me stuck in a "victim" mindset.

Creeping in with the "victim" mindset during this time, was allowing the pulmonary function test (PFT) results, which tell how my lungs function, define me. In my mind, my quality of life was only good if the numbers were good. All I focused on was getting my numbers to 90% of normal. Forget nutrition and exercise! If the numbers dropped below 90%, in my mind the world was ending and death was coming. The interesting part was when my numbers were at 90%, I didn't have more energy. In fact, I couldn't run and I often felt too lethargic to do anything fun.

Here's a secret that you're going to want to highlight and memorize: **true wholeness and health isn't confined to perfect numbers.** There's no feeling like that of being set free from the bondage of thinking that way. Overcoming a life of sickness and bondage, so you can finally live your life in true wholeness and health, will be one of the most faith and strength building roads you'll ever have to walk. It's not something that happens once and magically changes your life forever. You choose this road every day.

Wondering when your number will be up because of a disease is no way to live. Being afraid to even dream of a better life because you might never get there because you died too young is no way to live. Constantly battling the anxiety, the fear, the doubt, the stress and the sadness that often comes with the diagnosis of a life threatening disease is no way to live either. You were designed for something more. Parents—your child was designed for something more than a life of sickness, fear, and bondage!

I've learned a few things on this journey and in all honesty, I believe it's my moral obligation to share them with you. I promise to be vulnerable and not to sugar coat any part of my story so you have the freedom to be vulnerable with yourself as well. If you let me, we can embark on a journey together that will open up a world of true wholeness and health for you and your family…a world you may never have allowed yourself to dream about, until now.

But first, take a moment and let the following words sink into the depths of your soul:

The sickness that is in your life is not your fault.

Say those words every day until they are rooted in the depths of your heart. Look at yourself in the mirror, deep into your eyes and say those words out loud if you need to. Parents – *your child's sickness is not your fault either*, it is not there to punish you either. We accomplish nothing until we face this truth head on and embrace it. When you embrace that truth, your struggles can become your greatest blessings if you let them!

Now, fasten your seat belt because what you're about to discover are vital steps for living the life you want – a life of true wholeness – in sickness and in health!

The first stop on that discovery is how to conquer the fear.

CHAPTER 1

WHAT'S THERE TO FEAR ANYWAY?

"Courage is resistance to fear, mastery of fear, not absence of fear."
- Mark Twain

Have you ever woken up crying before? Not like, when you wake up, stub your toe and burst into tears or because you woke up on the wrong side of the bed. I mean when you opened your eyes you found tears streaming down your face as though you were crying in your dream, but you don't even remember exactly what you were dreaming about. Have you ever done that?

This has happened twice in my life so far. The most recent was on October 13, 2010, two days after losing our home to a fire that almost killed our dog. I remember waking up to a wet pillow and my eyes filled with tears. There in the darkness of the early morning while my husband and miracle dog, Ajah B, were still sleeping, all that I could do was to just sit there with a heavy heart pondering all that happened in the last forty eight hours. But the apartment fire story is for another time and place…I want to talk about the first time.

The first time tears welcomed me awake was in 1997—the year the reality and fear of dying from CF smacked me in the face. That year my friend, Donna, passed away; she died from CF. She had just graduated from high school.

Up until then, I never personally knew anyone who died from this disease. Death wasn't something that entered my mind much; at the age of fourteen I was pretty healthy. A few years prior Donna's death, she and I had ended up in the hospital at the same time. We were neighbors with our rooms next to each other.

Having her there made the lonely two week hospital stay more bearable, and we often called each other to talk late into the night after the nurses made us stay in our rooms for the evening. It was fun…well, as fun as a hospital stay can be. You learn to make the best out of being in the hospital if you're a frequent guest at "Club Med" as we called it. Donna and I also spent a week one summer together at a CF camp, long before they stopped CF kids from hanging out together because of viruses we could spread to each other.

News of Donna's death hit me pretty hard. The day I found out I was actually at the doctor's office—a month to the date after she had died. My doctor must have seen the hidden fear in my eyes because he walked over to me and said, "Mandy, that won't be you." Of all the words my doctor has ever spoken over me through the years, I've held onto those words of life with everything in me. Those were words I received with open arms, even though the fear never went away.

It was a few months after finding out about Donna that I woke up crying. Tears were spilling out of my eyes and I had a heavy heart. It was no surprise really. I remember looking at pictures of her last few days on earth; she was hunched over a pillow so she could breathe easier. That image of death stayed etched in my brain for fourteen years.

After internalizing what Donna must have gone through and how she died I had a dream about her and woke up crying. Her death was an event that opened the door to fear…and I let that fear move into the deep crevices of my heart; in a complete daze my hands gripped fear's bags and helped it unpack and make itself at home.

This wasn't on purpose, it just sort of happened. It stayed hidden there for years, only popping up to torment me whenever there was news of another friend dying from CF or whenever another trip to the hospital was scheduled. The fear was such a part of my heart that it began to kill my dreams.

As a child I had dreams of becoming a singer. I sang everywhere I went and I was proud to tell people that I was fighting CF and still able to sing. Celine Dion and Mariah Carey were my favorite singers, and I had visions of becoming just like them. When I was nineteen, I quit college and took time to record my first CD. During the song writing process, memories of the dream about Donna turned into a song about her called "Awakened Tears." It was an amazing experience. The thrill of being in a recording studio and hearing my songs come to life was one that words truly can't describe.

Shortly after my CD was released, my boyfriend proposed and we became engaged; so I took a job as a music secretary at our church. And then…the dreaming stopped.

Ask anyone living with a disease and they'll agree that they are warriors—constantly fighting to survive every day of their lives—but never free. I lived the first six years of my twenties in fear and bondage...well, maybe my entire life was lived that way. Fear and bondage to an invisible, insidious beast dwelling in my body—one that I had invited in! Oblivious to it at the time, I began believing the lies fear fed me. Because of this, being vulnerable with myself or anyone else was not an option.

Over the years I watched my parents get teary eyed many times when the time came for me to go to the hospital for a tune-up (the CF version of proper maintenance). I couldn't possibly let them know their courageous daughter was scared out of her mind and she was afraid she would never reach her dreams because of this disease. Camouflaging my insecurities seemed much easier. Paint a smile on my face and bury my fears deep inside. Ignore them and just live my life day by day.

Over time, my big dream of a career as a professional singer was traded for smaller, short-lived jobs that became careers I could conquer. But those jobs kept me feeling empty and after changing careers several times, the truth could no longer be avoided—fear was ruling my life.

Maybe you know the feeling of fear too. Maybe you live with a disease and understand the fear of it winning and you losing. Maybe you're scared for your child who has a disease. Have you ever stopped to ask yourself what the cause of that fear is? The fear that ruled my life was a voice in my head that sounded like this…

"Don't say that, what will they think if they knew the real you?"

"You can't possibly travel alone to a big city – someone might kidnap you, you could lose your medication or you could even get lost, then what would you do?"

"You shouldn't even try to start living your dreams because you're going to get sick before you ever reach them anyway."

"Oh no! You're lung functions are low again–this is the beginning of the end so brace yourself!"

"What if your life is nothing but a big wish that never comes true?"

"What if you're on the brink of living the life you want and then CF snatches it all from you?"

The voice was never a loud, shouting voice; it was a snarling whisper that fed a gentle panic that slowly rose until my nerves were so full of anxiety and defeat that I couldn't even think straight. It would quietly scream at me and remind me that the clock was ticking and soon my turn would come.

Fear is such a silly thing really. It's sneaky and it keeps us stuck. Fear keeps us sick or keeps us from moving forward into a healthier version of ourselves by tricking us into thinking that we are being "careful" when really we're just being fearful. Fear likes to mask the truth. It clouds our mind so we can't see any other possible outcomes other than bad ones.

But here's what fear doesn't want us to know: *fear can serve as a compass*. In fact, it's the best compass out there! If there's something you've always dreamed of doing but you're afraid of it, then you MUST do it because waiting on the other side of that fear is something that will equip you for your future.

Fear is conquered by faith; faith is usually sharpened by tribulations and trials. In fact, in the Bible we are told to rejoice in trials and tribulations because the testing of our faith produces perseverance (James 1). That doesn't sound like any fun initially, but out of the greatest trials in my life—like overcoming sickness and starting over after losing my home to a fire—those trials produced a confidence, a faith, and an attitude that, quite frankly, looks fear in the face and smacks it into hell! That quality alone is worth every ounce of fear that I ever felt so it could be overcome.

Maybe you've never heard of telling fear to go to hell. The first time those words hit my ears it was a bit of a shock, so no worries if you're in the same boat right now. Your Creator, God Almighty—your Father in Heaven—did not create you to live a life of fear. He tells us all the time in his word, "Do not be afraid." It doesn't matter whether or not you believe in God, he still loves you and you were designed for a life without fear.

Living your life in true wholeness and health requires that you must find the courage to identify your fears and face them head on. **To put it bluntly - fear has to die.**

My way usually involved a journal, soft music, and time locked away somewhere so I could think clearly. There were questions that needed to be answered in order for me to kill my own fear. Questions like…

What are you most afraid of?

Why are you afraid of this?

What would you do if you weren't afraid of this?

How would your life be different without this fear?

Some of the discoveries that showed up on my journal pages included fear of success, fear of failure, fear of what others think of me, fear of dying too young because of a disease, fear of making mistakes, fear that people won't like what I have to share, fear of not being good enough, fear of bad weather, fear of disasters, fear of discovering the real me that was hidden somewhere beneath my skin…there were a lot of fears there!

After identifying the fears, I had to find the courage to feel the intensity of each fear so I could recognize it in the future and conquer it. Usually we tend to shy away from feeling fear. We just stuff it away so we don't have to deal with the uncomfortable feelings.

What we fail to realize is that stuffing fear away just makes those feelings even more overwhelming. It makes us feel powerless and utterly hopeless. When we stuff our fears away, we rob ourselves of healing; fully feeling our fear is the beginning of healing. ***We must feel the fear to its very core.*** Journal about it; cry about it; scream over it…whatever needs to be done to let it all out, do it. Hiding and ignoring it will just make it grow and give it more power over you.

One evening while journaling about my own fears, a breakthrough happened. After I wrote the words "I'm afraid of dying of CF" on the page of my notebook, I burst into tears and spent the next hour crying hot, angry tears as images of Donna's last days reeled through my mind like a movie. Curled up in a ball on my bed, finally the wall had broken and I had allowed myself to face the fear.

Was fear gone forever? It would try to creep in again on cold winter days that burned my lungs or whenever a lonely night at the hospital happened…but now I knew what it felt like and I could battle it head on. *It no longer held me captive.* Eventually I learned fear is a spirit and all we need to do is tell it to go back to hell where it belongs in Jesus' name. Tell ya what…that's fun to do! It brings out boldness, that's for sure!

The funny thing about fear is we often don't realize it's gone and we've conquered it until we face another trial.

For instance, one summer we had a tornado warning in our city. My husband worked out of town two weeks every month so I was home alone with Ajah B., our shihtzu, when all of a sudden the sirens went off and the sky grew pitch black. We joined our neighbors in the underground parking garage and wondered what was going on outside as we heard the snarling wind and the pounding rains. Then, the electricity went out…and it stayed out for ten hours.

Now, had this happened a year ago, I must admit I would've been panicked and scared because I was alone in the dark…with nothing but my thoughts, the deafening silence, and my little ten pound dog who, quite frankly, wouldn't hurt a fly. My mind would have been filled with questions and fear over the possibility of losing our home or some of our belongings to a tornado. My imagination would have been on overload thinking there was someone in the apartment or ghosts or something. I watched lots of scary movies growing up, bad idea, I don't recommend that if you want to get rid of fear!

But this time, none of that happened. I was completely calm, even when I didn't have a flashlight or a candle. Thankfully, a new neighbor I had just met while taking shelter in the garage had brought me one of each.

Let me repeat that –

· the old fear of having strangers help me out was gone;
· the fear of losing belongings was gone;
· the fear of ghosts and creepy bad people breaking in was gone;
· the fear of being alone in a storm was gone!

I made a conscious choice that night to have faith and I told fear to go to hell where it belongs…and I was fine. Not only was I fine, but I was able to think clearly and strategize about how I would handle the electricity being out for longer than anticipated, if needed. Had I been scared, I wouldn't have been able to think at all!

Overcoming the fear of sickness will equip you to be fearless in other areas of your life too. Learn to master the skill of identifying, feeling and directing your fears. It's an important tool to have when overcoming sickness!

Once I overcame fear, I found a new perspective, which also opened a door to understand the power I had within my reach—my own words.

CHAPTER 2

A NEW PERSPECTIVE & WORDS OF LIFE

"The tongue has the power of life and death..." – Proverbs 18:21

By the time I was 26 years old, I had racked up quite a few statistics of my own. Obstacles in the form of daily pills, inhaled treatments, medical bills, and hours spent at the doctor or in the hospital piled up at my doorstep, with more added every morning. Here's what those statistics looked like:

· Consumed 250,000 pills

· Racked up $663,000 in medical bills

· Spent 14,235 hours doing treatments, roughly equal to 1.63 years of my life.

· Sat in 244 doctor appointments

· Spent 2,472 hours in the hospital for what the CF world calls "tune-ups"

These numbers are quite conservative because most CF warriors could double or even quadruple some of those numbers for the same number of years. It would be easy to dwell on the problems, don't you think? Come on, the medical bills alone would put some of us over the edge! But why do that? It would just be a waste of time and a waste of life really. What good is it going to do me or anyone else to spend time as the guest of honor at a pity party?

In order to see the gift in these obstacles, a new perspective was needed. Just add a few new letters from the alphabet, and obstacles became opportunities. Opportunities that made my entire situation seem more a blessing than a curse. Here's how it works.

- 250,000 pills = dedication and discipline to stay healthy and maintain life. This allowed me to make other healthy choices such as better nutrition, exercising, and getting enough rest.

- $663,000 in medical bills = helping pay someone else's salary and giving them job security! Hey, maybe there were some kids that were able to eat because of me, right?

- 14,235 hours doing treatments = personal reflection time. I learned how to spend time journaling and praying because I was forced to sit in one place for forty minutes at a time. This was also the beginning of learning to be more patient!

- 244 doctor appointments + 2,427 hours in the hospital = time to develop lifelong friendships with people I wouldn't have met otherwise. It even became time to inspire and encourage hospital staff who needed words of life spoken over them too.

The simple decision to shift my perspective also opened the door to learn the power of words. Out of the heart the mouth speaks. We find that in the Bible (Luke 6:45) and when you begin to pay attention to your own words and the words of others, it's not hard to see the truth of that statement. It's very possible to be a happy person and still speak words of death and focus on the wrong thing. That was me for the majority of my life.

Speaking words of life is something that should be taught in schools, churches, businesses...everywhere really. But it's not. Growing up we often heard, and probably even proclaimed, "Sticks and stones may break my bones but words can never hurt me." Big time false! **Words do hurt**, and we completely miss the importance of our words on a daily basis.

Hearing a doctor tell your parents that your daughter (you) probably won't live past ten years old hurts. Hearing and reading on the internet that people with the same disease that's in your body will probably die before they turn thirty hurts. Those words not only hurt, but they set your brain and body up for a constant fight. Your desire to be healthy or have a healthy child always pales in comparison to words that statistics speak, unless you shift your focus. Without that shift in perspective, a part of your hope dies, whether you realize it or not.

What do you focus on? In other words, what thoughts consume your mind, whether you want them to or not? Are you filled with thoughts of sickness, hopelessness, despair, or dead finances? Are you filled with thoughts of feeling run down or thoughts of giving up? Or, are you filled with thoughts of a long life? Are you filled with nagging thoughts that haunt you and bring anxiety or fear? Then your focus is on the wrong thing. You're speaking words of death—through the thoughts in your own mind—over yourself. It really is that simple.

Most of us have probably been surrounded at one time or another by people who speak negatively, gossip, and say conflicting words about us or over our lives constantly. If that's you, this is going to be one of the most challenging areas to overcome. But, you can do it! I struggled with this very thing for years, sometimes I still find myself struggling with it. Words of worry and doubt were spoken over my life often, many times from my very own mouth. Words of worry are words of death. They sound something like this:

"I hope I don't get the flu because my friend had it!"

"I can't go skiing with the youth group because I might get sick from being out in the cold too long."

"I never remember anything, I hope I don't get Alzheimer's someday!"

"How am I ever going to pay my bills with this medical debt?!"

Let's do a quick case study. Have you ever noticed what happens when you're around someone who is sick with the flu, a cold, or bronchitis—basically anything nasty that you don't want to catch? What happens? What do you normally say? Most people say things like, "I hope I don't catch that!" or "Stay away from me, I don't want to get your germs!"

Have you ever uttered those words? What usually happens when you do say those things? A few days later you most likely wind up just as sick, if not worse. Why did this happen? Because you focused on the negative; **you focused on what you didn't want** and you spoke what you did not want into existence, or you agreed with it when someone else spoke it over you.

If the life you are living is not what you want—your health isn't good enough, your finances aren't getting better, your marriage sucks, you hate your job, oh, and your kids don't listen—then you must begin to shift your perspective. Stop speaking things you don't want! That will only bring you more of what you don't want.

I spoke things into existence that didn't suit me for years and the result was years of colds and flus, three sinus surgeries, loneliness from not going on trips with my friends and feeling completely hopeless because things never seemed to happen the way they should. And then I chose to shift my perspective and speak words of life. Look at the difference now.

One afternoon my husband, Nate, and I went to a funeral with my in-laws. My brother-in-law was coughing the entire two hour round trip, and my husband and I were scrunched in the back seat with him. Every time he coughed, you could see us trying to inch ourselves further away from him. We had learned and implemented the skill of using our tongues for life by this point, but it was a battle to not speak death and sickness that day! I so badly wanted to say, "I better not get sick!" But I kept my mouth shut, and banished those thoughts to the pits of hell several times throughout the day.

Two days later we found out that my brother-in-law had a bad case of bronchitis! Yikes! Now, normally I would've been saying to my husband, "I better not get what he had!" and I would've ended up sick too. This time though, because both my husband and I had been practicing this skill, we looked at each other and said out loud, "Thank you Lord that we are healthy and strong!" And we didn't get sick.

This may seem completely crazy to you, and maybe you're tempted to stop reading right now. But what's ahead in the rest of this book could change your life forever!

Maybe you're in a situation where you've been focusing on the medical numbers and the statistics of your situation so much that you feel all hope is lost and all you can say is, "I don't want to get sick!"

Maybe you feel like your entire life hangs on the balance of those numbers. Living with CF or any other disease is filled with so many challenges, obstacles and unknown variables that it can consume you, if you let it. Every doctor appointment can become a life-altering milestone. If you let it.

Having the right frame of mind, the right focus, and aligning your words with where you want to go is critical for overcoming sickness so you can live a life of true wholeness. When this became real in my life, I made a choice to begin basing my health on my quality of life and how I felt instead of the number on a screen. I made a choice to reprogram my tongue and start speaking words of life instead of words of sickness, death and worry.

Something spiritual happened when this choice was made. It was as though my shift in focus brought about a new sense of faith and positivity that had been buried years before. All of a sudden I could do things that had been impossible before—like run a 5K and breathe outside in the middle of the winter without any chest pains. I could literally feel the presence and the peace of God in the room with me at every doctor appointment, even when the numbers got so low that statistically I should have been put on a lung transplant list. The choice to shift my perspective and speak life made the numbers irrelevant. Life was spoken over my circumstances and life prevailed!

What do you want for your life? What do you want for your child's life? If you want a life of sickness, worry, doubt, anxiety...keep focusing on what you've been focusing on. Keep speaking the words you've been speaking. But if you want something different, something better...then learn to tame your tongue, shift your perspective, and speak life.

If you're a parent of a child with a disease, people sometimes come up to you and say, "I never would have thought your daughter was battling a disease because she looks so healthy!" Instead of getting angry that they don't understand, thank them and say, "I receive those words of looking healthy you just spoke over my child!" And if you are a person of prayer, begin praying Bible verses and words of life over your child.

You choose which words you will allow to take root in your heart. Parents, you choose which words will paint the future for your child. Hard times will come. Kids will still get sick. But your choice to use your tongue for life instead of death will be a blessing and a strength to yourself and your child. It will be the difference between living in sickness and despair or living in true wholeness completely free of bondage no matter your circumstances!

In the next chapter, just like the words you use are a choice, you'll learn so is health.

CHAPTER 3

THE CHOICE TO BE HEALTHY

"Prevention is better than cure." – Desiderius Erasmus

Health is a choice. It goes beyond the cards you've been dealt in life. The very definition of health is the general condition of the body or mind with reference to soundness and vigor. What does vigor mean? It means active strength or force; physical health, mental energy or power.

Without health, life is pretty hard to live. That's a loaded statement when you're struggling every day to overcome a sickness. But what if there were some skills you could learn to help you have better health in spite of your current obstacles? Here's what my life looked like when health was not chosen.

There was a season during my junior year of high school where I decided to start exercising. Knowing that accountability was important, my best friend teamed up with me. The goal was to walk on the treadmill three times a week and start drinking more water.

Day one started out great. We both walked on the treadmill for thirty minutes and even did one hundred sit ups! When we were finished, we walked upstairs, grabbed a bottle of water and proceeded to sit on the couch with a brand new large bag of potato chips. In our defense, the chips were baked not deep fried. Of course, the fact that we finished off the entire bag in one sitting didn't exactly motivate us to keep up our healthy routine. So feeling defeated and guilty, we gave up and day two never happened.

Eating bags of potato chips wasn't a new habit for me back then. That was actually a normal snack. The diet of a CF patient is filled with high fat, high calorie foods. As a kid this was great because everyone let me eat as much candy and junk food as possible. No food was "off limits" because it was important for me to gain weight and keep it on, something quite challenging for most CF patients.

But feeding your body a constant stream of chips, sugar, soda, boxed food and high fructose corn syrup has less than desirable side effects. It's no surprise I was plagued with migraine headaches several times a month from fourth grade to well into my adult years.

During my twenties, in addition to the headaches, I had very little energy to do anything fun after a full day at the office. My life consisted of going to work, then come home, become a couch potato, watch my favorite television shows and then going to bed only to start the same boring routine all over again the next day. Weekends were filled with fun, sometimes, but also lots of sleeping because when my routine was interrupted it didn't sit well with my body. Plus, there were always those unbearable headaches that would visit me two to three times a week. Sickness seemed to be winning, with me slowly trying to catch up but feeling utterly helpless.

Have you ever felt that way? Maybe you feel that way right now. Prevention really is better than a cure, and the answer is actually right under our nose. It shouldn't be a surprise—we hear it all the time, including the skills we need to live healthier in the area of nutrition, exercise, and rest.

The year I turned twenty-six was the year this lesson started making sense. The time had come to get serious about my overall health, not just the parts affected by CF. I joined a gym and started working with a personal trainer so I would have accountability and someone there to make sure I didn't hurt myself. The first time I stepped on a treadmill as an adult, I couldn't go any faster than the speed of three without feeling winded and light headed, completely drained of all my energy. Now it's not uncommon for me to run on a treadmill for thirty minutes at speeds between 4.5 and 6 several times a week.

My personal trainer whipped me into shape through weight lifting and yoga...and then she tackled the area of nutrition. Nutrition is something most of us don't really like to think about, but it's so very important. It really makes or breaks our quality of life. We were designed to eat food from the earth, not food from a box.

Now, before you start to judge, understand that I grew up on home cooked meals as well as bagel bites, pop and cereal—I get that it's hard to even fathom eating things that don't come from boxes! But **health is a choice**. You may not be able to change the fact you or your child has a disease, but you definitely can improve their health and quality of life by what you put in their mouths as well as your own.

Every week that I met with my personal trainer, she required me to bring a detailed food diary. If there was anything in the diary full of caffeine, processed, or loaded with sugar, it would be circled in red. The first few weeks were tough! Everything was circled with thick red marker! My food diary looked something like this:

Breakfast: Starbucks latte and banana bread (if I ate at all)

Snack: diet coke and chips

Lunch: macaroni and cheese plus another diet coke

Snack: snicker bar and another diet coke (or skittles, cake, etc.)

Supper: pizza

Snack: chips and finally, another diet coke or a 7up

Obviously I was not feeding my body correctly and it's no small wonder headaches and fatigue plagued me so much! Here's the valuable lesson learned during this season of my life: feeding your body correctly means

- eating LOTS of fruits and vegetables,
- drinking lots of water, and
- getting enough protein.

Clinical research actually proves that eating a variety of fresh fruits and vegetables everyday will help reduce oxidative stress in your body and will also increase our cardiovascular wellness.

Do you understand anything about oxidative stress or cardiovascular wellness? It's okay if you don't, most people don't right away, myself included. I didn't even think it applied to me, but it does. It applies to you and your family too.

Basically, according to research, when you eat a wide variety of fruits and vegetables every single day you feel better, have more energy, have more endurance when you work out, you get sick less often, you have less stress in general and your overall quality of life improves! In terms of overcoming CF, more fruits and vegetables could ultimately mean less antibiotics because your immune system will eventually be able to fight off colds better than before you ate this way.

When my personal trainer first taught me this, I could only handle eating apples and grapes. Vegetables tasted horrible to me. But we have to start somewhere. I began by taking a quality supplement of fruits and vegetables in a capsule form so I wouldn't taste them. Not only did it give me more endurance and energy, but over time it helped me start to crave the vegetables I used to hate. Planning out my snacks helped too, and I would put one cup of grapes into a little ziplock baggy and bring a few bags with me to work to snack on throughout the day. Over time, there was less candy in my life and the headaches started to lessen.

Here's another tip. Protein shakes are great to drink because they are pretty easy to tolerate and digest and they give you the nutrients you need. Get creative! Put strawberries into your shake so you get more fruit. If you are really brave, have a vanilla shake with orange juice, frozen fruit, and spinach to add an extra serving of vegetables in your day. Spinach is a great source of calcium and it helps strengthen your lungs. You can't even taste the spinach in the shake, but it will probably look like something the Incredible Hulk® would drink! Be sure that you choose a good quality shake. Whole food shakes and supplements are truly the best choice.

After looking at my food diary, my personal trainer also challenged me to drink more water and less pop. You've probably heard this one your entire life too. Water is an essential part of our bodies. On average, you should drink half your body weight in ounces of water a day. However, if you are working out, you need to double that. This was a little trickier for me to overcome, as you'll see.

Growing up, my dad loved to restore old pop machines with glass bottles in them. It was a fun hobby, and as a kid it was like living in a soda shop. This is where my soda addiction started. Water was not something that ever entered my mouth; it was something to shower in or wash the dishes with.

Maybe you feel the same way. If so, here's a trick you can start with—it worked wonders for me. Begin with flavored water, not the carbonated water for it will only remind you of soda. If you really can't handle the taste of water, just start with flavored water. Your mind will be tricked into thinking its real water because it will be clear, and it won't be carbonated or thick like most juices. Then, add one regular bottle of water a day. Eventually you will work yourself up to having the amount of water you need.

By the end of my season of working out with a personal trainer, my food diary only had one red circle per week, the. Starbucks I made the conscious choice to reward myself with each week! The results from exercising, from running and yoga, were amazing. My lung functions improved and my energy levels picked up, too. Between the exercise and the healthier food choices, my strength and energy were higher than they had ever been. To this day, running is a huge part of my health maintenance. It's not abnormal for me to run seven to ten miles each week.

But not everyone is a runner. So if running isn't your thing, shift focus a bit and work on simply moving more. Moving more can be as simple as choosing to take the stairs instead of the elevator, or you can choose to park your car further away from the door to walk further. If you like being outside, then take a thirty minute walk every day. Go for a walk around the block with your spouse or kids, or take your dog for a walk. Moving more does not have to be some giant task where the thought of it makes you tired and worn out before you even tie your shoe laces.

You can do this. Moving can be fun and whatever makes you move more is the perfect thing for you to do.

The other skill in choosing health is rest. We can't ignore this one. Remember, health is a choice and sleep is just as important as nutrition and exercise. It's especially important when your body is healing from sickness.

I spent years skimping on rest. My life was lived like the Energizer Bunny® until I crashed so hard it put me in the hospital. I tried to do everything without enough rest. At one point in my life I was working a full-time forty hour a week job, building a part-time business, acting as the Women's Event Coordinator for our church, helping the music ministry, and trying to strengthen my marriage—all at the same time. Oh, did

I forget to mention I did all of that on top of spending twenty hours a week just trying to maintain my health through rigorous treatments and medication? Yep, that lifestyle ended me in the hospital, on several occasions.

Everything changed when I hired a business coach. She lovingly pointed out that my lifestyle was sucking the life out of me. She challenged me to scale back on several things—less volunteering, only five hours of building my business a week, spend more time with my husband...and get enough rest.

Most people need seven to eight hours of sleep each night to function at their capacity. Very few can thrive on six hours of sleep and some people actually need nine hours of sleep, but not many. Here's the exception to how sleep works. If your body is going through any type of healing process or emotional stress, whether it's from a surgery, a change in medication, any type of infections you might be fighting or even a circumstance that was overwhelming and stressful, you will need more sleep. The trick is not to fight it. Embrace rest because you will come out stronger and more energized on the other side, if you give yourself grace and listen to your body when it tells you it needs to rest.

Ask any pregnant woman and she will tell you that her body requires more sleep than she ever imagined during the pregnancy. Why? Because the process of pregnancy takes so much more energy. The same goes for the process of healing and choosing better health. If sleep wasn't important, we would not be designed for it. It's that simple.

Seven hours of sleep seems to be the magic number for me. If I'm sick or stressed out, it might be closer to eight hours. Here's what happens when I have less than seven hours of sleep—I cough, wheeze and feel tired all day long. Plus, I get crabby, irritable, and overwhelmed easily. It's not fun. Maybe you can relate?

A few years ago my husband and I started implementing one day of rest every week. We were amazed at how much better our lives were. For a while, our day of rest was always Sunday. Now we have to be more flexible because our work days fluctuate.

Here's what a day of rest does NOT look like. Get up at 7 a.m. to get ready for volunteering at the church. After church is over go out and spend lunch with friends and family or have them over to your house to enjoy the meal you threw together before you went to church. Come home and clean the house—scrub the toilets, dust the furniture, vacuum the floors, wash the clothes, and maybe spend time organizing the garage. Help the kids with homework and run them all over town to see their friends. Spend some time going through the family finances. Hurry up and do the grocery shopping plus put it all away. Oh yes, and remember to give the dog a bath and then get everyone ready for bed and then fall into bed yourself out of breath wishing you had more time to just relax and rest but that will have to fit in...next year.

That is not a day of rest. That's a day of work, and if you have too much of that type of work in one week, you're going to drop dead from exhaustion and full of regret because you didn't enjoy life. I'm not saying you can't go to church or do something fun with your family and friends. I'm saying pay attention to what you want your life to look like, and make sure you get enough rest so you can actually live your life and enjoy it!

Our day of rest looks like this. We wake up without an alarm clock. It's true—we sleep until we wake up. We spend time reading the Bible and praising our God and Savior. We might have breakfast at Starbucks or we might make it a brunch instead depending on what time we woke up. If we are in town we go to church. Sometimes we spend lunch with family or friends, but not often because our day of rest is a day for us to be together without any strings attached. We play games, go for walks, read books, watch movies, take naps...very low key activities that we normally don't do during the week. You won't find me cleaning my house or working in my office or on the computer on a day of rest. In fact, the only time a computer is touched on a day of rest is to watch a movie or to Skype™ with friends. I don't typically "do" my hair or makeup either. We stay in our pajamas and just...relax!

Because of this day of rest every week, we both have more energy, feel more fulfilled, I'm not as worn out anymore, and we get way more done during the week. Plus, we feel more connected as husband and wife because we spend time with each other instead of being slaves to the expectations of others or the tasks of the world. There's nothing better than a day of rest after a busy week!

You don't have to hire a personal trainer or a coach to get these results in your life too. If accountability motivates you to do better, you can hire someone if you want to or partner with a friend who wants a life of true wholeness and better health too. Just remember that health is a choice and making better choices is going to be a process. Healing takes time and so does implementing new habits!

Starting these new health habits reveal places within us where we need to choose a beautiful path to get to true wellness—that is the path of forgiveness.

CHAPTER 4

A BEAUTIFUL PATH CALLED FORGIVENESS

"The weak can never forgive. Forgiveness is the attribute of the strong." - Mohandas Gandhi

The white lights twinkled behind the head table. Soft music and the sound of silverware on china echoed through the room as the wedding party entered the ballroom. Over four hundred people were attending this elaborate wedding. As the hotel wedding planner, it was my job to check in with the bride and groom and make sure everything was going well. It still amazed me that even after two hundred weddings, the excitement of socializing with the crowd still put an extra skip in my step.

This particular wedding was extra special. Not only was it one of the last weddings I would manage before leaving my position at the hotel, it was also filled with the familiar faces of the people who lived in my hometown. I strolled up to the cash bar and started chatting with people I had not seen in years.

Suddenly one gentleman, who was quite drunk already, recognized me and exclaimed loudly, "Wow! You're still alive?!"

It was more of a question than a statement. Shocked at the words I was hearing, I steadied my weight on one leg and crossed my arms as he finished his thought, "I thought you would've been dead by now from that thing you live with...what is it called again?"

Nervously I cleared my throat, "Cystic fibrosis." He nodded his head as he took another sip of his beer. I put on the biggest smile I could and sarcastically answered, "Nope—I'm still here!" He didn't seem to notice my answer.

Irritated by his nerve and complete lack of tact, I spun around and left the ballroom. I stuffed the anger, hurt, and resentment deep down inside and pretended like it never happened. At twenty-five years old, I hadn't learned the full value of forgiveness.

Forgiveness is a powerful thing. In fact, it's so powerful and so simple that most of us don't even realize it is a tool we can use to improve the quality of our lives. Often it's the most important tool. Research has proven that the ability to forgive can begin the process of healing from many terminal diseases such as cancer, lupus, and even crohn's disease, to name a few. What I'm about to say isn't scientifically proven, yet, but I am going to be so bold as to say this—forgiveness can even open the door to healing from cystic fibrosis. Why would I say that forgiveness could heal a disease for which there is no cure? Because I'm living proof of it, that's why.

Most of my life was spent in a protective mode. Yes, there were many moments of happiness and laughter, but when the conversation would turn to the life expectancy of someone with cystic fibrosis, I would get fidgety and somewhat anxious. I'd even avoid looking the person in the eye. That was a topic I would rather pretend didn't exist, and through the years began to build up resentment and judgment toward anyone who dared speak those words in my direction.

I especially began to *resent and judge myself* because I was the one who ultimately had to live with such a thing. Admitting this is not easy for me, in fact it's probably a surprise to those who know me best because I have always been the first to speak positively about living with CF. But here's the thing, as I found the courage to dig deeper, this is the type of stuff that came up —the truth about how I thought about myself and others. It wasn't pretty, and quite frankly, it was keeping me stuck and sick.

There were years of resentments and judgments built up in the deep corners of my heart. Some of the examples I am about to share may even sound familiar to you.

In fourth grade, a fellow student came up to me and said something that made me resent her for years. She told me she read in an encyclopedia (the internet wasn't around yet) that I was going to die before I was thirty years old because people with CF don't live past the age of thirty. Yes, she actually said those words, and in such a matter of fact way that when she was done, she just shrugged her shoulders and walked away. I'm pretty sure that I just rolled my eyes and vowed to never be her friend again. I did my best not to let it bother me, but the words got in and somewhere, deep inside, those words took root and became heavy baggage I took with me everywhere. Out of the root grew the fruit of unforgiveness, a fruit that continued growing for years.

In high school, I fell completely head-over-heels in love with a classmate I barely knew. He had a very athletic build with gorgeous blue eyes and a talent for always saying charming things. All of those amazing attributes couldn't hide the fact that he saw me as someone who was different—someone who was and always would be limited by CF. He once made a statement that he didn't expect me to be able to keep up with him in any athletic capacity because of my condition. Ouch! That hurt more than I realized and I kept the resentment and pain of those words hidden in my heart for a decade.

College came with an interesting turn of events. The first month was awesome—my roommate and I got along so well you would've thought we were best friends since grade school. Then, something changed. Out of nowhere, she started treating me differently and even began to claim my treatments were making her sick. She asked me not to do treatments when she was in the room.

In an attempt to be a good roommate, I started doing my treatments when she was gone and opened windows to vent the medication smell better. The only problem was that after a while, she never left. So I started skipping treatments more often. Eventually, after three months, the anxiety of living with a difficult roommate and the lack of treatments led me to the brink of going in the hospital. I added this incident to my already growing pile of resentment and unforgiveness.

It would be great to say my twenties were filled with bliss and dreams come true. There was some of that, yes, but there were also more moments of resentment and judgment building up and ruling my life. I avoided the "well-meaning" distant relatives that would remind me of my condition by saying, "Mandy, in your condition you can't afford to get sick!" Insert rolling of the eyes here please! I avoided the people who would constantly ask how I'm "feeling" instead of getting to know me as a person.

I got married to Nate at the age of twenty. Three years into our marriage I ended up in the hospital twice within six months. My CF Center at the time was three hours away, so Nate stayed home to work while I went to "get better" at the hospital. The first time I went in, he wasn't able to visit because of his work schedule; the second time, he wasn't able to visit because he put his back out of place and was ordered to stay home by his doctor. I remember telling him I understood, but deep down I was hurt, scared and wanted nothing more except for him to be my knight in shining armor and leave his schedule to rescue me. That didn't happen; thus adding more resentment, judgment and unforgiveness.

It was around the age of twenty-three I started believing the words of death and limitations people spoke over me. I stopped dreaming big and I gave up on my plans of being a singer and inspirational speaker. I figured it was best not to dream—at least then I wouldn't be let down. I started going after smaller goals that seemed more attainable. That left me feeling worthless and empty, and out of those feelings grew resentment, judgment and unforgiveness toward myself.

Do you see a pattern here? Every single time someone said or did something that made me feel inferior or reminded me of CF, I would get offended and begin to resent them and judge them. The biggest person I held resentment, judgment and unforgiveness toward though—was myself!

I held myself in bondage because I wasn't healthy enough or strong enough. I wasn't good enough in my own eyes because I believed the words people said about and to me. I wouldn't even allow myself to be vulnerable enough to see what I was doing to myself. So, I ended up in the hospital, felt depressed and just didn't think my life would be any better so I should just be thankful for what I have and what I've been able to do because that's as good as it was going to get.

But then in 2009, forgiveness entered my life.

Then I started on a path that completely changed me and how I lived life. Seriously, I don't even recognize the girl I was, the girl you just read stories about, because that's no longer who I am. I learned the value of extending forgiveness, and the freedom that comes with it.

Over the course of twelve months, I began forgiving those who had hurt me. I forgave the grade school classmate who spoke those horrible words over my life. I forgave the ex-boyfriend who broke my heart and made me feel inferior. I forgave my college roommate. I forgave my husband. I forgave the distant relatives and the acquaintances who knew me growing up. I forgave everyone that came to mind when I reminisced about the hurtful words that kept me stuck for most of my life.

And then I forgave myself.

Here's something to remember about forgiveness—it's not a onetime thing. In fact, many days I had to forgive the same people over and over because there was still something that irked me when a memory popped in my head of what they said or did! But over time, an amazing thing happened, the resentment and the judgments were gone, because I had truly forgiven.

Ironically, when I ran my first ever 5K race, the very first person to congratulate me after crossing the finish line was the girl who said that horrible thing to me back in grade school! My excitement over the accomplishment of running the entire 5K race, with no pain in thirty seven minutes, took over and before I could stop, we found ourselves embracing in a giant bear hug! Recognizing the irony of this chance meeting, I thanked her for the encouragement. She was a little bit stunned I think.

In all honesty, though, the hardest person for me to forgive was myself. I held myself to such a high standard that every time I made a mistake, got sick, or failed to hit a goal, I would resent myself more until finally my self-confidence was so low I felt like a constant failure. I started living in the "fake it 'til you make it" world until that finally crashed too. There's no true wholeness in being fake! I had to come face-to-face with my unforgiveness…and once I did, and started practicing daily forgiveness, the chains were crushed and I began experiencing wholeness and health like I never knew.

I'll never forget the day that I looked in the mirror—straight into my own eyes–and said out loud, "Mandy, I forgive you for giving up and for thinking you weren't good enough. I forgive you for the years you believed the words of death spoken over your life and I forgive you for not believing in yourself. I forgive you, I release, and I bless you…and I renounce all judgments I have toward you. I'm proud of you, Mandy, and you're going to make it. You are good enough!"

To my surprise, big tears started rolling down my cheeks and I cried for several minutes after that. And then I felt lighter—I had truly been able to forgive myself and I was ready to move forward with my destiny.

Since beginning the daily practice of forgiveness, my health and quality of life have improved more than I ever could have imagined. I know there is no way I'd be able to run several miles a week, or even live the amazing life I live now, if I still held on to the resentment and judgments that used to weigh me down. I definitely wouldn't be able to share my life with you and inspire you if I still held on to all that crap!

Forgiveness is serious stuff! It must become a daily part of our lives if we want to succeed. Until the day we die, people will say or do things that hurt us. The great news is we can choose if we're going to let that slow us down or not. We don't have to carry the baggage with us everywhere we go. We can choose the beautiful path of forgiveness, the first step to walk by faith and not by sight.

CHAPTER 5

WALK BY FAITH, NOT BY SIGHT

"We must walk consciously only part way toward our goal, and then leap in the dark to our success." – Henry David Thoreau

According to dictionary.com, faith has the following definitions:

- Confidence or trust in a person or thing
- Belief that is not based on proof
- Belief in god or in the doctrines or teachings of religion

To say that I am a woman of faith is somewhat of an understatement. I have so much faith I'm willing to risk my pride and ego for the faith I have. I guess you could say I've always been this way. As a child, I had a very overactive imagination. In fact, it was so overactive that I spent my days with my invisible twin sister. Her name was Melissa. She was sent away when we were in fifth grade. I don't recall why. *wink*

Being raised in a Christian home, there was never any question in my mind Jesus could heal me and someday he would. In seventh grade I attended a youth conference with our church youth group. The evangelist got up on stage the last morning of the conference and he said, "I don't know who you are, or what you have, but there is a young girl here who was born with a disease—you have to take lots of medication every day—God wants to heal you." The moment he started speaking, I knew that he was talking about me because my body instantly felt different. I was way up in the balcony, and I had never even met this speaker, but as he spoke I felt a tingly sensation that started in the tips of my toes that went all the way up my body and out the top of my head. I instantly started shaking and crying, but I was too embarrassed to go up to the stage. So, my youth group leader and friends prayed for me right then and there. There was no medical documentation that said I was cured of CF, but from that point on I stayed out of the hospital for eleven years.

Several years later, in college, I was at a college retreat and that same speaker was there. This time he spoke words over my life that nobody but God could have known what I was thinking, struggling with or praying for. My faith was strengthened and since then I've exercised my faith and allowed it to be challenged, whether I look like a fool or not.

I learned from one of my mentors, Dani Johnson, to ask God for anything because he tells us to in the Bible in Mark 11:24. When the reality of what God says in the Bible was revealed to me, I began testing it out…on the weather. No joke! I figured, "What's the harm of having faith that God can change the weather if I ask him to?" So that's what I asked for on several occasions.

The first time I asked was on a cruise ship in December 2009. The weather was warm, but it was cloudy more than it was sunny. I thought I would just test it out, so as I was reading my Bible and praying on the deck one afternoon, I asked God to move the clouds so the sun could shine on us—and while he was at it, it would be great to see a dolphin too! I said the prayer and then I started reading my book.

No less than ten minutes later, the sun was shining directly on the ship and following us as we cruised across the ocean. Clouds were everywhere in the sky, except for on the ship! Then, I noticed something in the water that looked like some sort of fish—a whole school of them actually. There, before my very eyes, were not one, but twelve dolphins!

The second time I decided to try this was several months later at my uncle's wedding in Estes Park, Colorado. As the vocalist for his outside wedding, I was waiting for the sound guy to get his equipment set up so we could do a sound check.

It was in the middle of a terrible rainstorm, windy, rainy, and cold with no sign of sun anywhere in the near future.

I stood there shaking my finger at the wind and reminding God that he promised we could ask for anything, so this weather has got to stop and the sun must shine! In Jesus' name! Sure enough...the storm stopped and the sun came out and shined for the rest of the afternoon and evening.

Why am I telling you these stories and what on earth does faith have to do with true wholeness and health? Faith has everything to do with true wholeness and health. In Hebrews 11:1 we read "Faith is being sure of what we hope for, and certain of what we do not see."

What are you hoping for right now? Do you hope for it **and** believe it will happen? Or are you hoping for it and believing it will never happen to you?

Faith is something that must be exercised every day, whether we see proof of it or not. Here's a personal confession. I have faith God has healed me of cystic fibrosis, even if I don't see it from a medical standpoint.

I exercise that faith every single time I run—and I run four to six times a week for two or more miles at a time with no pain, no gasping for air, and no feeling like I'm going to pass out like several years ago. I am taking less medication than before, and if I get a cold, my body is able to fight it off on its own with no medication, or at the very least, far less medication than years ago because my immune system is stronger than it has ever been before. My body digests food with fewer enzymes than it used to and even though there may be times when my lung functions are low, I feel better than when my lung functions were at their highest! I have faith that God is doing something in my body that cannot be explained by medical science.

What do you have faith in?

This might be shocking you right now and it might even be something you are skeptical of or even shy away from. Can I tell you something? If you don't believe in God or healing or anything like that, it's okay. I'm not going to judge you. I will tell you that you do have faith whether you believe in God or not.

You have faith that the food you eat is going to nourish your body. You have faith that when you turn on the switch to the light bulb it will shine and give you light. You have faith that the wind can blow through the trees even if you can't see the wind with your own eyes. You don't have to believe in God to have faith, but you might actually be surprised at what will happen if you start having faith in God and exercise that faith by speaking his words of truth over your life.

God's word—the Bible—is full of so many nuggets that can literally transform your life, if you start to speak them and believe them every day. I will put my faith in God's word long before I put my faith in medicine. Is there a place for medicine and does it work? Yes, absolutely. But too often we as humans tend to believe more in medicine than in the power of God and his word. That has got to change if you are serious about living your life in true wholeness and health!

I'm not saying you should run away from medicine and scorn it; I'm saying it's time to rise up and exercise your faith and your belief in God's word. Allow him to transform your soul and your DNA as you breathe life over your circumstances through his words of truth. Partner your faith with medicine and see what God does.

One of the things that has become a part of my daily routine is speaking God's words of truth out loud over my body and my circumstances. Marker boards with Bible verses written on them are everywhere in my home so I can see them every day. Anytime I feel sick or hopeless, I speak Bible verses over my body and my faith grows—so does my boldness.

Take some time and digest the following words of truth, and then write them down on a marker board or on your mirror so that you can see them every day. I dare you to start speaking them, out loud, over your health and your circumstances!

Proverbs 4:20-22

"My son, pay attention to what I say; listen closely to my words. Do not let them out of your sight, keep them within your heart; for they are life to those who find them and health to a man's whole body."

Proverbs 18:21

"The tongue has the power of life and death, and those who love it will eat its fruit."

Proverbs 9:11

"For through me your days will be many, and years will be added to your life."

Isaiah 46:4

"Even to your old age and gray hairs I am he, I am he who will sustain you. I have made you and I will carry you; I will sustain you and I will rescue you."

Isaiah 54:17

"No weapon formed against you shall prosper, and you will refute every tongue that accuses you."

1 Peter 2:24

"He himself bore our sins in his body on the tree, so we might die to sins and live for righteousness; by his wounds you have been healed."

John 14:12-14

"I tell you the truth, anyone who has faith in me will do what I have been doing. He will do even greater things than these because I am going to the Father. And I will do whatever you ask in my name; so that the son may bring glory to the Father. You may ask me for anything in my name and I will do it."

Hebrews 10:35

"So do not throw away your confidence; it will be richly rewarded."

Hebrews 10:39

"But we are not of those who shrink back and are destroyed, but of those who believe and are saved."

John 15:5

"I am the vine, you are the branches. If a man remains in me and I in him, he will bear much fruit; apart from me you can do nothing."

Philippians 4:13

"I can do all things through Christ who strengthens me."

Isaiah 7:9

"If you do not stand firm in your faith, you will not stand at all."

CHAPTER 6

COLORING OUTSIDE THE LINES

"Everything is always impossible before it works." – R. Hunt Greene

The year was 2003 and the pain shot up and down my back like sizzling knives. It made me dizzy and exhausted. Muscles in my lower back contracted so tightly that the only solution to stop the pain was to dive to the floor and lay flat on my back for what I hoped would be fast relief. This was my first experience with horrible, almost crippling back pain. Having heard stories of other back pain sufferers, it was clear that my future would include lots more suffering. Instead of viewing regular chiropractic visits as a preventative means, my method was to wait until the pain was so bad and the muscles so stiff that someone would need to help me walk around, or until my body was so obviously crooked that it couldn't be ignored anymore.

No one really explained the connection between disease, health and chiropractic care and to ask the question never crossed my mind. So for the next seven years, chiropractic was only an option if walking was not possible. Prevention and wellness did not coexist in my brain yet.

This next statement might seem a bit...unorthodox. Consider it anyway, because your reaction to it could possibly change your or your child's life. Are you willing to color outside the lines of traditional medicine and the majority of the world's mindset in order to have a better quality of life? Don't misinterpret that—it doesn't mean give up and ignore traditional medicine altogether. It means partnering the traditional with natural methods so that your body isn't immune to medicine when you need them most.

If someone would have asked me that question back in 2003, my answer would have been "no way!" It's no small wonder that there was so much fear inside of me. I was afraid to do anything that my doctor did not believe in or agree with.

Many times throughout my life, a certain well-meaning family member would try to get me to use the latest and greatest natural product on the market or some strange concoction to help me stop coughing. This loved one took it so far as to writing my doctor a letter, basically telling him what he should do to help my case. In an attempt to keep me from harm, my parents were told to never give me anything without checking with him first.

Not bad advice...just not great advice for a risk taker like myself. It stifled me and made me leery of anything labeled "natural" or "organic." It stopped me from researching other health therapies for years. In fact, if the woman from 2003 still lived in this body today, you wouldn't be reading this book. But, here we are.

The skill on how to partner traditional medicine with natural remedies was something I stumbled upon really. It started from a desire to make more money and share my passion for overcoming obstacles with other people. In 2008, my entrepreneurial spirit partnered with the boldness that was rising up within me. The idea to color outside the lines of my current circumstances came because of starting a home business.

It sounded like a fabulous idea at first, but the truth was, some skills were missing from my repertoire. Skills necessary to succeed in building a business. There was no choice but to seek answers and what I discovered started me on a path that completely changed me from the inside out—both physically, spiritually, and mentally—especially mentally.

Do you know that having a closed mind is not a good thing? If you don't, it's not. It keeps us small and stifles our God-given abilities and talents. Obviously we don't want to be so open-minded and free-thinking that our convictions and beliefs change like the wind. But we need to be open-minded and willing to learn from others and not judge. We can learn something from every single person we meet, whether they are higher or lower than us on the social status scale. There's always more than one way to skin a cat! We must humble ourselves and choose to learn something in every situation. Starting a business humbled me. And it opened the door to a lifestyle of coloring outside the lines.

I was introduced to a company that sold fruits and vegetables in a capsule and after researching and getting a solid understanding of what was in the product, it seemed like a great idea to add it to my lifestyle. After just two months of taking the product every day, my results were so amazing that there was no question this was the company and the industry for me.

Working inside the wellness industry opened my eyes to a whole new world. It provided an entirely new outlook to many approaches that I had previously avoided and seemed scary. Over time, a much better comprehension developed about how natural health methods could help someone like me have a better quality of life.

You owe it to yourself, and your family, to look into what else you can implement, other than just considering more medication. Too much medication isn't always a good thing. Partnering traditional medicine with natural methods can be very beneficial. Don't just take my word for it though. Do your own research and decide for yourself. Keep all of these solutions in mind when you do.

Would you consider it crazy to visit a chiropractor once or twice a week? What if it improved your lifestyle by fifty percent? So much of our health is directly correlated to our nervous system and if any part of our body is out of alignment, we're not going to feel well. This was not something that crossed my mind in 2003. Honestly, this seemed completely nutsy to me! Isn't it funny how we view something as "crazy" when we have no real experience to back it up?

As an example, a chance encounter with a young chiropractor with new technology changed my point of view. He was a member of my networking group in 2009. We shared our stories over lunch one afternoon and suddenly there was no denying how important regular chiropractic care was. My first session with Dr. Barton consisted of x-rays, spinal scans, and an in depth conversation of what my lifestyle was like and where I wanted it to go.

It was refreshing to have a wellness professional be so passionate about my health goals. Of course, it's no surprise that the spinal scans showed my body was not on a path to lifelong health. Bars of red, black, and even missing bars indicated severe subluxations in my spine, which is when one or more bones in your spine get out of place and create pressure, that directly correlated to the function of my respiratory and digestive systems. In a nutshell, any health complications from CF were not going to get better without chiropractic intervention.

Over the next eighteen months, the wellness team at Dr. Barton's office became my weekly dose of encouragement along with the constant reminder the journey from sickness to health is a process. Many times when symptoms of a cold would appear, my gut instinct would be to call my medical doctor and start an antibiotic treatment ASAP. After experiencing chiropractic care, my new instinct is to get adjusted. What happened when I chose to get adjusted versus jolting my system with an antibiotic fix? My body recovered from the cold without antibiotics, and in many cases the cold never shows up at all. There have also been days where I'm coughing a lot but can't seem to cough strong enough to clear out whatever is in my lungs. Immediately after an adjustment my breathing gets better, the cough gets better, and it eventually lessens or stops as the day goes on.

Chiropractic care is one of my secret weapons for a life of true wholeness. Do your research, interview a few chiropractors to find the best one for you, and see what happens. But don't just stop there...

Picture yourself on a beach. The sound of waves crashing on the shore, the smell of sea air, and the touch of a gentle breeze filling your senses as you enjoy a pampering massage in a private cabana. Sounds relaxing doesn't it? But let's get real—how many of us only consider a massage as a special treat while on vacation? Some of us never consider a massage at all!

Regular massage is another perfect way to color outside the lines of traditional medical routines. Massages, sauna treatments, reflexology, and even essential oils are all methods that can help overcome sickness and relieve stress. Each of these methods have helped strengthen my immune system, get rid of toxins in my body that had built up over time, and promote an overall stronger body.

What is it that you are searching for today? Maybe you're searching for an answer to fewer medications for you or your child. Maybe you're searching for relief from headaches, colds, back pain, or stress. Maybe you've never stopped to think about what you're looking for, you just know something is missing.

You're not alone. Once upon a time that was me. All I know is that God Almighty works in mysterious ways. Sometimes people receive instant miracles. Sometimes healing is a process. Sometimes the answer is right in front of us, waiting for us to step out in faith and grab hold of it.

Have you been fearful or judgmental toward new ways of thinking and alternative, natural methods of health? It's okay if you have. Forgive yourself, and choose to start a new path today. Begin to color outside the lines. Research the methods shared here. Start implementing new habits in your day to erase the thoughts of doubt, fear, worry and skepticism that have plagued you for so long. Coloring outside the lines is a process, one best suited for individuals completely committed to improving the quality of their own lives and the lives of their loved ones.

You might be wondering how you can start coloring outside of the lines right away. How about this—turn off the television! Pick up a book and learn a new skill. Listen to authors, wellness professionals, and entrepreneurs who inspire you to be more, do more, and have more. Shut the door on judgment and choose to learn as much as you can. Be selective about what information goes into your brain and the brain of your kids. You're never going to be able to implement new habits if you don't get rid of the voices that tell you it can't work, it's stupid, why are you doing this, etc.

Coloring outside the lines reaches beyond your physical wellness routines. Are you ready for another secret weapon? Program your mind while you sleep by listening to audios. This is something Nate and I do every night. We listen to the Bible when we sleep. Some people choose to listen to audio books or coaching classes, and that's great too. We listen to the Bible because we've found that the more we listen to God's living word as we sleep, the more it becomes a part of us. We're not only reading his word every day in our private devotions, we're hearing it for seven to eight hours each night! There's no easier way I know of to reprogram your mind for positive thoughts than to listen to God's word as you sleep. It's like a soothing lullaby.

By the way, God tells us throughout the Bible to pay attention to our thoughts. In fact, in the book of Haggai—a small little book of only two chapters—God tells us five times to "Give careful thought to your ways." Five times he says this in two short chapters! Don't take my word for it. Grab your Bible and check it out for yourself.

Our entire world is a result of our thoughts. If you don't think anything in this book will work for you, it won't. But if you are willing to set aside negative thinking and judgment to try something new, your world will be rocked by the nuggets shared in these pages—including how to keep going and growing in the next chapter!

So...there's only one question left to ask you in this chapter. Will you keep coloring perfectly the way you always have or are you ready to color outside of your lines?

CHAPTER 7

NEVER STOP LEARNING, NEVER STOP GROWING

"There are people who take the heart out of you, and there are people who put it back." – Elizabeth David

"Something has to change, Mandy! We can't keep doing the same thing over and over again expecting a different result!" Dani Johnson's words resonated deep within me on that evening of February 3, 2010.

Dani is a multi-millionaire business trainer whom I had been learning from for eleven months and every single thing she said cut to the depths of my soul like a double-edged sword. I so desperately needed to hear what she was teaching, even if it hurt my pride a little bit...okay, most of the time it hurt my pride a lot because I had a HUGE ego. Dani had the courage to tell me what I needed to hear in order to grow into the woman that God designed me to be. That evening, I learned more about myself than ever before.

One of roughly fifty students in Dani's accountability class, the time had come to stop sitting on the fence and get to work. This was a serious class with an investment of $2,000 and the possibility of getting kicked out if your homework wasn't emailed in on time. The entire focus of the class was to help us develop our skills in business, debt, and time management. My stomach churned with butterflies as I dialed *2 on my phone to raise my hand and ask a question.

"Okay, Mandy Anderson...how can I help you tonight?" asked Dani.

"Well," I started out softly—almost too quiet to even hear myself ask the question that, in my mind, seemed to have no answer, "I have a hard time managing my home business with my life and I have a tendency to make myself sick because I'm doing too much."

Over the next several moments I explained how my life consisted of working full-time in a new position at a hotel and being stressed out because this brand new position was designed specifically for my skillset. On top of all the "newness," I wanted to keep building my home business ten hours a week. After taking time off from my home business because of a hospital stay a few months earlier, I was ready to dive in again head first and get this thing figured out!

"So, what you have is a very stressful full-time new job that requires a learning curve," Dani began to explain. "You just got out of the hospital because you wore yourself out and stretched yourself too thin. Prior to going into the hospital you were working forty hours a week plus an additional eight to ten hours per week on your home business. So…eight to ten hours per week plus forty hours per week equals two weeks in the hospital. Do you see the recipe?"

Deep breath. Her words slowly sunk in. Honestly, it had never occurred to me to look at the recipe before and no one had ever taken the time to sit down with me and point it out.

"So you got out of the hospital and now you want to go BACK to ten hours per week!" Dani exclaimed with a compassionate chuckle that eased the tension and confusion oozing out of me and into the phone line. "We still have the full time job, still have CF, still have ten hours per week and we still have a tendency of doing that to yourself! Something has to change, Mandy! We can't keep doing the same thing over and over again expecting a different result. You are a beautiful, intelligent woman and never in a million years would I have ever thought that you had this thing—CF—going on with your body. So here's what we're going to do…"

Dani went on to help me craft a schedule that was doable for my lifestyle while still working towards my dreams. She also pointed out to me that I needed more fun in my life because there was too much intensity in my world.

"Since you 'fight' this disease every day, it means you are fighting most of your life. There needs to be to a point of release in having some fun," she compassionately explained. "We're going to make it to the finish line alive! Alive would be good, Mandy—not suffering with pain, not two weeks in the hospital. We're going to train for the marathon, not the sprint. Let's get you healed and healthy!"

It seems so funny to be sharing this story with you. Thinking back to that evening, it never crossed my mind that her words would be such a profound message that would carry over into the lives of others as well. Have you ever stopped to look at the recipe going on in your own life?

Every single successful person has had to face their demons. That's what makes them successful. Learning how to face what haunts you and knowing what to do so you can overcome is one of the most valuable skills to possess. There's nothing more important than continuing to learn and grow on our journey. We were never designed to stay the same. We were designed to succeed, to be healed, to make a difference and to leave a legacy for others to learn from.

When we wake up one day and find that our dreams have been stomped out of our hearts because of our circumstances or because people crushed our spirits, our next step is to find someone who has what we want and begin to learn from them.

It's the only way to get back up and overcome the obstacles that keep winning.

Until the moment Dani pointed out how much "fighting" was going on in my life, I had no clue that's what I was doing. Being vulnerable enough to even admit there was something agitating me from deep inside my brain every single day seemed way too frightening. The moment she said it though, a bolt of peace surged through my entire body. Finally that "thing" that was inside of me—the thing that kept wearing me down day in and day out—was identified. It was the fight. The fight to breathe, the fight to live, the fight to prove others wrong, the fight to beat the clock...the fight to be me.

Maybe you've felt that same fight within yourself. Maybe you've been yearning to feel a surge of peace bolt throughout your own body. Maybe you're ready to find a mentor who will help you discover what's holding you back so you can finally rise up and become the person you've always dreamed of being. Those visions you see inside your head are there for a reason. They are proof of what's to come, IF you seek out a mentor and are willing to go through the refinement process so you can receive it.

The job of a mentor is to push us outside of our comfort zone and point out the habits that keep us stuck in life. Few mentors truly have the courage to shine light on the tough things. A great mentor will love you enough to say things that at times will make you mad and offend you. His or her job is to shine a light on the locked doors of your heart covered in cobwebs so you can finally do the spring cleaning you've been avoiding for years.

It's not easy to be vulnerable with yourself when you're born with a disease, or when you're the parent of a child that has a disease. It's much easier to just go through the motions of living and pretend like nothing is wrong. It's much easier to give up and give in to the people who say it can't be done or it won't work. Telling the voices of worry, fear, and doubt to shut up and go back to hell where they belong requires tremendous strength and if we don't have someone encouraging us along the way, we're more likely to quit. Mentors have a way of encouraging us and lighting a fire under our butts at the same time!

The moment we become stagnant and stop learning is the moment that we have lost the race. When our days become nothing more than endless treatments, medication, and the same old routines with no sense of adventure, growth, or dreams then we are merely existing while at the same time stifling the true wholeness that screams to get out.

Let's put the color back into our lives. Let's promise each other, and ourselves, to keep growing no matter how painful the discoveries are. Let's resolve to seek out a mentor that will love us enough to tell us the truth so that we can dig out the roots of all the weeds that choke us out, which opens the door to our destiny.

CHAPTER 8

OWN YOUR DESTINY

"You define your own life. Don't let other people write your script."
- Oprah

There's a book filled with historical story after story about regular people accomplishing extraordinary things in the midst of ridicule, slander, and uncertainty. In it, there's a guy named Noah who built an ark when rain had never even been heard of. People would walk past him every day and question his work. They'd tell him he was crazy, wasting his time, and that nothing would ever come of it. Of course, if you're familiar with this book called the Bible, you know that rain did come, and because of his faithfulness and belief, Noah and his family were the only people that survived the great flood that consumed the entire earth.

Then there's the story of Nehemiah. He had a dream of rebuilding the wall around the city of Jerusalem. He sought God and was given favor to accomplish this dream. He was ridiculed a lot; pretty much every day. What's so astonishing about Nehemiah is his character. He knew and understood the power of his words, putting things into action and keeping his eye on the mark.

When city officials mocked him, he kindly reminded them God would give him and his workers success. And when Nehemiah found out those very same officials had plans to destroy his hard work, he just ignored it and kept working. He protected his dream by resolving to keep going. He wasn't distracted by the taunts of naysayers. He wasn't discouraged by the fact that others disagreed with him. *He just kept going* and in his lifetime he saw the fruit of his labor when the wall was finished.

What do these stories have to do with living a life of true wholeness? And more importantly, what do they have to do with overcoming sickness? Both Noah and Nehemiah had a calling on their lives. They each had a dream that they had to fulfill and they weren't going to let anyone stop them. That same determination must be present in our lives if we are serious about overcoming sickness and any other obstacle that rears its ugly head.

So often we have dreams in our heads and think they're just going to fall out of the sky and into our laps. We have believed the fairytales that say everyone will love us and no one will ever disagree with us when we start to live our dreams. That couldn't be further from the truth. When you make the decision to rise up and go after a life of true wholeness—when you decide to overcome sickness, fear, and doubt—you must expect that opposition is right around the corner. So you must protect your decision to rise up. You must protect everything that it takes to get there. **You must own your destiny!**

Nehemiah owned his destiny when he told his adversaries God will bless his work, even if it didn't look like it would be blessed at that moment. Noah owned his destiny when he focused on obeying God's instructions so the boat wouldn't leak! You're going to have to own yours too, if you plan on overcoming your obstacles. You're the only thing standing in your way.

Ask any one of my friends from grade school and high school and they'll probably tell you it seemed like I owned my destiny. Some of them would probably say that I lived in a misguided fantasy world. The old me would probably agree that I did live in a fantasy world. Call it what you will—fantasy, big dreaming, escaping from reality—either way, my passion for beating the odds and accomplishing something big in my life was proof of the faith that resided deep within my soul. It was also proof, in advance, that someday I would indeed own my destiny.

Maybe you're wondering what it means to own your destiny. What do you do when you own a new car? You treat it with special care. You're proud of it and excited to share it with everyone you know, right? You wouldn't dare think of belittling it because you worked so hard to get it. You would stand up for the reasons why you bought that model instead of something else. You would do everything possible to make sure no one keyed it, messed it up, stole it or broke into it. You wouldn't take it for granted because you would understand the important role it played in your life. You would handle it with care because you understood how powerful a machine it really was and you would not dare to park it and never drive it. You would want to use it all the time!

It's the same with owning your destiny. That passion that keeps you up at night...that dream that brings tears to your eyes...*that calling on your life must be handled with care*. The desire you have for a better quality of life is proof that you are supposed to have a better quality of life. Handle that desire with care. Own it as though it were the most expensive car you've ever laid eyes on!

Owning your destiny does not mean you give in to a life of sickness or the death sentence of a disease. It means you rise up and do the best you can to live your God-given dreams *in spite of a disease*. How many of us have been inspired by stories of people overcoming insurmountable odds? How about the story of Helen Keller? She could have given in to a life of loneliness. She could have been someone we never heard of because she just accepted her disabilities. But no, she owned her destiny.

She fought through the difficulties of learning how to communicate in spite of the hindrance of being deaf and blind. What seemed impossible to everyone else became a story that has inspired generations since then.

What is it you are dreaming of? What destiny have you been waiting to own? Maybe you've been staring out the window of a hospital bed for so long that you can't even remember what you thought your purpose was. Maybe you've been fighting for the survival of your child so much that you've lost sight of yourself. Maybe you've dreamt of being a teacher but your health would be at risk if you did. Guess what—it's never too late to start owning your destiny. Start right where you are at!

When you decide to own your destiny, remember to water your sprouts so they can grow. A sprout, according to Dani Johnson, is proof of what's been planted and evidence of what's to come. The trick is to not stomp on your sprouts. Learn from my mistakes...

Back in 2002, instead of celebrating the fact that my dream of recording a CD had been accomplished, I belittled it by believing the voices in my head that said I'd never make it as a singer because of my health. Single handedly the ownership of my dream was handed over to the voice of mediocrity and the father of lies. The result was six years of trying to hide from the destiny that haunted me until it finally had to be dug up and reharvested.

Every single time I ended up in the hospital, the sprouts of getting better would be stomped on by me saying things like "Yeah, well, your lung functions would be flying high too if all you got accomplished was four treatments a day." or "It's not going to stay that way when I get out of here because there's no way I'm living a life confined to that many treatments every single day." The determination to not live a life of treatments was good to have, but it was smothered by stomping on the sprout of having such amazing lung functions while in the hospital.

Remember, the words we speak create our reality and they are either giving life to our harvest or killing it.

Every single lesson shared in this book is a potential sprout for you. It's a seed for you to start your own harvest. As you begin to implement the lessons learned here, you're going to find there will be moments where you feel helpless, lost, lonely, and even moments when you'll be attacked for wanting to create a different lifestyle for yourself and your family. ***Protect those sprouts by choosing to speak life.*** Protect those sprouts by choosing to be selective about who you hang around with and what you listen to or even watch on television.

If you don't protect your dreams of a better lifestyle, no one else will do it for you. If you don't choose to own your destiny, no one else will make you. In fact, most everyone else will do their best to keep you where you are. They'll tempt you to stick with your old habits instead of incorporating new ones that will make you happier and healthier. It might sound a bit mean, but you might have to find some new friends to keep you on the right path as you walk towards the destiny that haunts you.

Protect your sprouts of facing your fears. Protect your sprouts of speaking life instead of death. Protect your sprouts of choosing to eat healthier. Protect your sprouts of practicing forgiveness. Protect your sprouts of walking by faith and not by sight. Protect your sprouts of coloring outside the lines and using natural health methods with traditional medicine. Protect your sprouts of being mentored by someone who cares enough to lift you out of the ash heap you find yourself in.

It might cost you some friends…oh well. It might cost you your pride…good! Too much ego will just keep you blinded and stuck anyway. Learn to protect your sprouts and embrace your destiny. You're the only one who has ownership rights to your specific destiny so rise up and own it…whether you live in sickness or in health, it is a journey of a little bit, every day.

CHAPTER 9

A LITTLE BIT, EVERY DAY

"We know only too well that what we are doing is nothing more than a drop in the ocean. But if the drop were not there, the ocean would be missing something."– Mother Teresa

The morning session was starting and people scurried to their seats as a woman with dark brown hair and tanned skin walked to the front of the room and took her place by the podium. Her yellow shirt with white capris was the perfect outfit on a beautiful summer day, but they also spoke of her confidence and authenticity. I opened up my notebook, put my black and green pens on the table, and took a sip of my coffee.

"Take consistent action every single day or a year from now," Kathrine began saying "part of your belief will have died." A burst of energy surged throughout my body as I heard her say those words. So that's what that feeling was every time there was a lack of consistency in my life. It was my belief slowly dying. My hand jotted down her words quickly and I was eager to catch the next phrase that came out of her mouth.

Kathrine Lee made a decision sixteen years prior to be consistent in working her home business, every day. She weighed 300 pounds at the time, had a two year old, and was juggling her bills every month. Her decision to work one to two hours per day consistently paid off. Sixteen years later she has lost 175 pounds, had the luxury of raising her kids while working from home, and built her business to the point of having financial freedom while helping others do the same. Her real life example of consistency and her weight-loss story created such a buzz she appeared on the Oprah show three times. Here she was standing before a room full of people sharing her wisdom. There was no way any of her words were going to escape my grasp!

Consistency.

The dictionary defines consistency as "steadfast adherence to the same principles, course, form." Hmm...that sounds great and all, but how does that apply in real life? Maybe you've wondered what that means for your life too. Consistency is something that used to be a struggle for me, or so I thought. The truth was I knew how to be consistent, had done it many times throughout my life, but during my adult years my consistency seemed to be directed at the wrong thing.

Growing up with CF, consistency was something that came easy. My parents taught me early on to keep a routine. Every day certain things had to take place—do breathing treatments, take pills, do everything possible to not get sick, and call the doctor immediately if a cold or the flu seemed to be on the way. Doing all of these tasks at the same time every day made it so much easier to live a normal life.

But then...I became an adult with the new challenge of juggling the consistency of taking care of my health with going after my dreams at the same time. This is where I dropped the ball.

Instead of applying consistency in the new area of going after my destiny and owning it, I made the choice to give up on my dreams and to focus only on living the consistency of life with a disease. A life-threatening disease at that. Here's the part I missed for about seven years—no matter what our circumstances are, we were not made to give up and give in to sickness, debt, bad relationships, or whatever messes seem to follow us around. Just because our health requires a little bit more care than the average "normal" person, doesn't mean we can't continually go after our dreams. Our dreams are there for a reason and whether we are living in sickness or in health, they are meant to be lived and not just dreamed about.

Well, I was notorious for consistently having big dreams and then sitting on the couch waiting for them to happen. Guess you could say I lived in the land of "no common sense." Seriously. In my mind, I believed the lie that said someday I would be pumping gas at a gas station and singing a song when low and behold some talented agent would find me and sign me up to become a singer right then and there. Yep, I really believed that my dreams would appear with no effort of my own.

The thing about believing that lie was this—every single day thoughts of what could be popped into my head and like clockwork, I consistently pushed them aside by listening to the little gremlins on my shoulder screaming "you can't do that— you're nothing but a sick person destined to die young! Stop dreaming! Stop trying! Give up! Give in! Just hook yourself up to your vest and do your breathing treatment again and STOP DREAMING!"

It's kind of funny to think how consistent I was with entertaining such lies! The lies finally became so uncomfortable a change had to happen. That change started with a decision. The decision to stop being consistent about watching television, eating chips, and wishing my life away. The decision to stop consistently believing the statistics that said I would die before I was thirty—actually, to just stop paying attention to the statistics altogether!

I made a decision to start being consistent with reprograming my brain for success, reprogramming my body for health, and consistently going after the destiny that haunted me every day. Once that decision was made to be consistent with entertaining thoughts of life and consistently doing the work to get to my dreams while staying healthy, my entire life changed!

This may seem redundant, but repetition is the mother of skill so it's important to hear it all again as you learn these new skills. It started with slowly changing my eating habits, shared in chapter three. Then, walking and running became more of a routine. Before I knew it, every day I was doing a little bit more to get me to my goals. Once my body and my immune system became consistently stronger, I was able to start working on my brain and ultimately, my skills.

For three years, I consistently learned from some of the best trainers in the world to get the skills to do what I wanted to do. As the Director of Public Relations at the Staybridge Suites, it was my mission to practice the skill of putting others first and speaking their language. So after two years of consistently talking to other people a little bit every day, not about myself, but about them, it was no longer difficult to put my pride aside and speak the language of the person my attention was focused on. It happened so swiftly and yet so gradually that I didn't even notice it. Someone else had to point it out to me. That's what happens when we do a little bit, every day. Eventually, the things we consistently do, little by little, become such a part of us that we don't even have to think about it anymore.

Maybe you're a parent and you just got the news your baby girl has cystic fibrosis. Maybe you're the patient and you're navigating through the emotions, the rage, and the uncertainty of your daily routine. Wherever you are right now, choose to be consistent.

Parents, consistently tell your children every day they can choose how to react to their circumstances. Consistently build them up, teach them how to take care of themselves, and consistently paint a picture of how they can reach their dreams, even in sickness. Consistently put your new habits and skills into action. Do a little bit every day. Don't expect to swallow it all at once or you'll gag; even worse, you might choke! Small steps every day are the key to lasting results.

A year from now is coming. You might write this day down in your journal and maybe have some great goals listed for next year. The truth of the matter is, if you don't do something every day—just a little bit to get you there—you'll be in the same spot a year from now that you are right now.

If you want to someday run a marathon or a 5K, but people say you can't, ignore their doubt and start going toward it today. Start by walking around the block every day. Little by little, increase your distance. Then, start running the length of a block and walk again. Be consistent. Get up when you don't think you can. Little by little start attacking with what you can do!

Do you have a desire to teach or inspire people? Why not start a business online? Start a weekly Facebook group and begin teaching there. Take classes and coaching to strengthen your skill. Stop using sickness as your excuse and do what you can right where you are at—right there in that hospital bed if you have to!

Stop accepting defeat. Stop giving up so easily and choose to be consistent every day and little by little you'll build the path to true wholeness. There's nothing like the feeling of seeing your consistent work pay off. Nothing.

Just moments before crossing the finish line of running my first 5K, tears filled my eyes. As cowbells rang and people cheered me on, memories of the consistent steps that had been applied for two solid years flashed before my eyes. Every small victory helped me accomplish a goal that never seemed possible. But little by little my consistency and hard work paid off, and in spite of being born with a life threatening lung disease...I ran a race and finished!

Where do you want to be a year from now? If we don't take consistent action, every day, part of our belief will die. Our belief in who we were meant to be, belief things can be different and better, belief in why we are here...our belief in making sure that others will be able to overcome sickness too because we had the courage to consistently rise up every day. Don't let your belief die. Rise up and be consistent day in and day out. Because a year from now is coming...

CHAPTER 10

TAKE A DEEP BREATH!

"We are the hurdles we leap to be ourselves." – Michael McClure

"Looks like you did it again. Every time you set a goal for yourself, you just fall short of the finish line. Guess you shouldn't be surprised...it's not like you're supposed to do anything important with your life for real. Remember when you wanted to become a singer? What happened with that dream? Oh yeah, you flew all the way to Chicago to try out for American Idol only to waste fifteen hours of your life waiting in line. The thirty seconds you had to prove yourself as a talented individual were not enough and once again you failed. Plus, you coughed all day long and who wants to listen to that?

"Remember that book you tried to write in seventh grade? What was it...a murder mystery book? Yeah, you got to chapter seven and just gave up. Remember when you recorded your CD? You gave up on that too. You give up all the time, Mandy. That's who you are—a quitter. That's just what you do. You give it your best until you get bored or sick and then you move on to the next thing telling yourself you don't care anymore.

"When are you going to learn?

"Oh, and don't forget your Starbucks habit! You say you have a passion for health yet you can't give up your addiction to lattes. What kind of a role model are you? Oh, and then there's the whole thing about mixing naturopathic care with traditional medicine. That's just a recipe for disaster according to anyone who knows anything about medicine. What are you doing? You are crazy. You are not worth it. And tomorrow you're going to have to forgive yourself all over again because you mess up all the time.

"Mandy, just give up. This lifestyle is much too tiring and you're not cut out for it."

Ouch. Ever heard phrases like that in your own head before? Those were just a few of the words that plagued me day in and day out. As I mentioned earlier, I was my own worst critic. Maybe you can relate. Maybe the voices in your head have left you feeling dizzy and defeated too.

Take a deep breath and let it all out. Feel the air filling your lungs and marvel in the miracle of life. This too shall pass!

Taking a deep breath and reminding yourself to extend some grace is a bit challenging. Extending grace to others can be a stretch sometimes; extending it to yourself can be a bear!

But...it's absolutely necessary in order to be free and live in true wholeness. It's still challenging nonetheless.

Remember to extend yourself grace when...

WHAT'S THERE TO FEAR ANYWAY?

Knowing what to do with fear and actually doing it are two totally different things. When first learning this skill, there were moments of pure frustration. Fear would set in and instead of directing it, I would entertain it and started to unpack its bags again. Then I would think, "Mandy, you know better than to pay attention to fear! What is wrong with you?!" The voice would scream at me and make me feel completely powerless to do anything. Completely frozen in fear and self-condemnation, I would do nothing but stare at the fear and let it mock me while I cowered beneath the covers in the dark. But then...I remembered to take a deep breath and extend some grace.

Learning a new skill takes time. We shouldn't condemn ourselves because we don't ace the test the first time around. On your journey, fear will set in. There will be moments where you drop the ball and forget where your courage comes from. There will be moments where you fear the disease that courses through your DNA. There will be moments where you panic and fear what your child's future might look like.

It's okay. Remember, you know what to do with the fear now. Take a deep breath and give yourself some grace.

A NEW PERSPECTIVE & WORDS OF LIFE

Every now and then, about once a week to be completely honest, my husband calls me on the words that come flying out of my mouth. In the middle of venting about something or talking my way through a situation, I'll slip and speak words of death instead of words of life. I'll sow a crappy seed. It's to the point now where the moment it comes out, I notice it and do my best to fix it, but Nate is great at keeping me accountable too. He'll look at me and say "just gonna point this out; you spoke words of death, Mandy."

I wish I could say my response to him is wrapped in words of appreciation...that's usually not the case. My typical response is to stutter and try to figure out what sort of excuse will work. Excuses never work, I know this, and so I end up going into another room to collect my thoughts and then calmly walk back into the room and thank my husband for having the courage to point out my mistake so I could grow and become better. It's quite humbling.

But what happens in my head, I agree with him and I sit there condemning myself even more. But then...I take a deep breath and extend grace.

A lifetime of sowing and receiving negativity doesn't go away in a moment. Neither does a lifetime of sowing seeds of worry and words like "I hope I don't get sick!" It takes time. There will be days when your focus is directed on the wrong thing. There will be moments where you panic and think you're getting sick and even speak the words out loud. There will be moments where you agree with the statistics and start to cower under the pressure of overcoming an impossible disease. It's okay.

Nobody is perfect and nobody gets this right the first time around. It takes practice. So...take a deep breath and extend yourself grace.

THE CHOICE TO BE HEALTHY

Sigh. Nothing compares to the feeling of sipping a hot, grande soy caramel macchiato at Starbucks. It's not good for me, it's true. In all reality, I choose to keep this in my lifestyle because it's something that brings enjoyment. Not sure why, but it's one of my favorite things to do—sip coffee, people watch, have a good conversation with a friend, or just journal and write a book. All with my cup of coffee. There's no way this would be acceptable for me without grace.

The journey from sickness to health is filled with so many moments of triumph, as well as pain. Overcoming a lifetime of bad eating habits isn't going to happen overnight. Overcoming a lifetime of never exercising and not getting enough rest isn't going to happen overnight. It takes time. You owe it to your body to give it the time it needs to grow stronger, if you're serious about living in true wholeness.

There's a healthier version of yourself waiting to appear. Take a deep breath and give yourself some grace! Allow yourself the ability to eat a favorite treat every now and then. Allow yourself the ability to stay up late one night, just for fun.

Healthy habits are not meant to be so stringent that you can't live. Take a deep breath and extend yourself some grace!

THE BEAUTIFUL PATH CALLED FORGIVENESS

The hardest person to forgive is yourself. It's hard to forgive yourself for being sick, for not having the physical strength to do normal things, for not having the mental fortitude to overcome the hurdle that stops you from moving forward, for not having perfect genes that kept your child from having a disease that seems to be threatening her very existence every day. It's hard...but it's not impossible.

Breathe. Extend yourself some grace and forgiveness right now. We live on planet earth, and forgiveness will need to be extended until the end of time because that's how God designed it. It's much easier to forgive when you have Jesus Christ in your heart, but even if you don't you can still walk in forgiveness.

Remember, you might have to forgive the same person for the same thing for days in a row. It's okay, that doesn't mean that something is wrong with you. It just means that the wound was deep and you need to keep practicing forgiveness every day.

Take a deep breath and extend yourself some grace!

WALK BY FAITH, NOT BY SIGHT

There's a true story in the Bible about Peter and Jesus. Jesus was walking on water one night and his friends were scared because they didn't realize at first it was him. Peter told Jesus that if it really was him, then Peter himself would be able to walk on water. So Jesus told him to walk toward him and Peter took a giant leap of faith and started walking on water himself. And then he looked down at the water and started sinking. Jesus all of a sudden appears at his side and says "Oh you of little faith."

If you've ever heard this story before, then you're familiar with how it is normally taught. Every time I've heard it told, there seemed to be an underlying condemning tone to it. But there is no condemnation for those who believe in Christ Jesus. So, what if Jesus was actually excited that Peter had a tiny bit of faith? He exercised what he had, and then he lapsed. You might feel the same way when you start exercising your faith. It's okay.

Walking by faith takes practice. Every time you step out in faith and see a positive result, your faith will grow. Don't condemn yourself for getting it wrong. Celebrate the fact that you exercised the tiny bit of faith that you had!

Take a deep breath and extend yourself some grace!

COLORING OUTSIDE THE LINES

Breaking free from coloring inside the lines takes time. It's only natural to want to dive back into your comfort zone when things get uncomfortable. If you choose to partner traditional medicine with natural methods, give yourself some grace and expect things to take a while to get used to. It's a process. Completely changing your routine is never easy—it takes a toll on you both physically and mentally.

Take a deep breath and extend yourself some grace!

NEVER STOP LEARNING, NEVER STOP GROWING

Mentors are going to push you. They will push every button you have to see if you will crack. When you do crack, it's okay. Cracking is the only way to let the seed inside grow. Cracking is good. You want to crack.

Take a deep breath and extend yourself some grace!

OWN YOUR DESTINY

Establishing the authority as the proud new owner of your destiny will not happen overnight. It's going to feel strange at first. From time to time you might even feel undeserving or unworthy of the destiny you dream of.

Write this next sentence in big letters and put it someplace you can see every day. YOU ARE WORTH IT! Take a deep breath and embrace this new adventure with grace!

A LITTLE BIT EVERY DAY

Remember consistency is more important than instant gratification. We live in a society where we are used to getting everything handed to us on a silver platter in the blink of an eye. That mindset has set all of us up for failure before we even start. You didn't arrive in this world a day after being conceived. It took nine months to get you ready to enter life on this planet. Rise above the mediocre mindset that plagues the rest of the world.

Take a deep, breath and be consistent with the right things every single day. Little by little...remember?

TAKE A DEEP BREATH!

Sometimes you can do everything right, and your health still declines. Sometimes you can make every change possible and things don't seem to improve the way you intended. Sometimes the hour glass runs out of sand before you have the chance to implement what you want to do. I don't know why life happens that way, all I know is that no matter what situation you're in right now, grace always helps.

Give yourself some grace, some mercy...in other words, stop being so hard on yourself. You're doing a good job. You're doing the best you can and you're determined enough to keep going. Give yourself some grace. Celebrate what you've done right. Celebrate where you've come from and where you are now. Celebrate the life that God gave you, the dreams, the pain, the loss, the tears of joy.

Celebrate it all and give yourself the grace needed to be able to take a deep breath. Enjoy the life you've been given and choose to be thankful. You get to choose if your life will be lived in sickness...or in health!

CONCLUSION

THE STORY OF YOU

"You have a gift that only you can give the world—that's the whole reason you're on the planet. Use your precious energy to build a magnificent life that really is attainable. The miracle of your existence calls for celebration every day." – Oprah

Now that you've heard my story, I'd like to ask you what your story is.

It's no accident you picked this book to read. Think about what it took to get this book into your hands. For one thing, it took me getting over my fears and insecurities so that this story could be shared. It took doing the work—facing the pain and heartache so that these pages could be written. Hours were devoted to editing, gathering testimonials, and researching the best methods to get this book out into the marketplace. And then, it took you making the decision to sit down and read through these pages, all the way to this very page.

This isn't a book for you to just walk away and think "that was a good story." This book is a guide, a road map, for you to model and start moving toward the life you've always dreamed of having. Forget the circumstances you find yourself in. Forget the voices that tell you to stop trying because you're too sick, too stupid, or too poor to do so. You are meant to reach your dreams. You are meant to succeed and share your story with the world around you.

Your next step is to take out a journal or a notebook, turn the page, and go through the exercises so you can get there too. So you can help your child get there too.

And when you finish the exercises, **share with me the number one thing you plan on implementing in your life**. Visit my website at www.mandybanderson.com and share your story so together we can impact the lives of others who are in the same situation! **Someone needs to hear your story of rising above sickness to true wholeness so they can find hope like you just did!**

It's not impossible. You were designed for this life of true wholeness that keeps whispering in your ear. I believe in you and I know you can do it!

I look forward to hearing from you. Until then…

Be blessed! Be healthy! Be inspired!

Mandy

YOUR NEXT STEP

CHAPTER 1 – WHAT'S THERE TO FEAR ANYWAY?

Identify Your Fears:

Write down in the space below, or in your own journal, what you are most fearful of at this very moment.

Feel the Fear:

Feel it – be honest enough with yourself and brave enough to look it in the eyes and stare it down. How does it make you feel? Does it make you want to cry, scream, binge eat? Write down the answer and spend some time allowing yourself to feel the full effect of the fear.

Tell Fear Where To Go and Map Out A New Plan:

· "Fear of _____, I am done with you! Go back to hell where you belong…in Jesus' name!" Tell it to go to hell and then dig a little deeper to find out what's underneath the fear. Map out a new plan to get outside of the fear.

- Ask yourself "why am I afraid of this?" (Here's a secret. When answering this question, you're going to be tempted to say "I don't know." That's taking the easy way out and leads nowhere. I'm here to help you thru. The way to conquer the temptation of answering "I don't know" and ignoring it, is to answer this question open and honestly: what if you DID know?)

Take it one step further and write down the answer to these questions:

- If I wasn't afraid of this...what would I do?
- How would I live my life if I wasn't afraid of this?

CHAPTER 2 – A NEW PERSPECTIVE & WORDS OF LIFE

Areas of improvement - write down 3 areas of your life that you want to improve:

1._____
2._____
3._____

Now take a moment and write down 3 things you are thankful for:

1._____
2._____
3._____

What are 3 negative things you say often? Write them down and then write a positive thing you can begin saying instead!

1._____

2._____

3._____

CHAPTER 3 – THE CHOICE TO BE HEALTHY

Nutrition

Write down a food diary of everything you've eaten today. Circle everything that is processed or full of caffeine.

·   Breakfast:

_____

·   Snack:

_____

·   Lunch:

_____

·   Snack:

_____

·   Dinner:

_____

·   Snack:

_____

Now look at it. Are there any raw fruits and vegetables on that list? Is there any water?

Now circle the things that apply to how your body feels right now, and feel free to add anything else:

- Slightly tired
- I could take a long nap I'm so exhausted
- My body has aches and pains
- I have a slight headache
- Wide awake and full of energy!

What nutritional supplements could you possibly add to your lifestyle?

Rest

Write down how much sleep you got this week and how you felt the next day.

· <u>Monday</u> – total hours of sleep = _____

· How I felt during the day = _____

_____

· <u>Tuesday</u> – total hours of sleep = _____
· How I felt during the day = _____

_____

<u>Wednesday</u> – total hours of sleep = _____
How I felt during the day = _____

_____

<u>Thursday</u> – total hours of sleep = _____

· How I felt during the day = _____

_____

- <u>Friday</u> – total hours of sleep = _____
- How I felt during the day = _____

_____

- <u>Saturday</u> – total hours of sleep = _____
- How I felt during the day = _____

_____

Sunday – total hours of sleep = _____

- How I felt during the day = _____

_____

CHAPTER 4 – A BEAUTIFUL PATH CALLED FORGIVENESS

Practice forgiveness by doing the following exercise every day:

- Search your heart right now. Ask yourself "Who do I need to forgive today?" and write down the first name that pops into your head. _____.

- Spend some time forgiving that person, release them from the judgment you had and even pray a blessing over them.

Remember:

1. If a name pops into your head and you've already forgiven that person, search a little deeper and forgive them again. That person is coming to your mind for a reason so take the time to forgive them fully!

2. If the name that pops into your head is your own, spend some time forgiving yourself and then begin to list the things that you really are proud of yourself for doing. Celebrate the things you do well, or the things you are learning, and forgive yourself for the mistakes you've made.

You may find that you have to do this many days in a row, toward the same person for the same offenses, before you begin to "feel" lighter, or before you feel like you could bump into that person with a smile on your face. Forgiveness takes time, so release yourself from the expectation of getting it perfect. As silly and strange as this may seem, the truth is you won't experience true wholeness and health if you skip this. It's a vital part of living your destiny so practice forgiveness every single day!

CHAPTER 5 – WALK BY FAITH, NOT BY SIGHT

Spend some time writing down Bible verses on your mirror, on a piece of paper on your fridge, or even on a marker board that sits in the hallway so that you can begin to see these verses every day. Refer to chapter 5 for Bible verses or write down your own. Speak them over your life daily!

CHAPTER 6 – COLORING OUTSIDE THE LINES

- Make a list of wellness professionals that you can learn from or start going to (chiropractors, massage therapists, reflexologists, etc.)
- What authors inspire you?
- Make a commitment to watch less TV and listen to audios that feed your brain.

CHAPTER 7 – NEVER STOP LEARNING, NEVER STOP GROWING

Find a Mentor

· Who is someone that you really admire?
· Who inspires you to accomplish your dreams?
· Who has something that you want?

Mandy B. Anderson has tools available to help mentor you on your path to True Wholeness. Be sure to visit www.mandybanderson.com for free training in spiritual growth, health and wellness, and overcoming sickness. Stay plugged in and connect with Mandy daily on Facebook and Twitter.

Below is a list of authors and mentors that have inspired and helped shape Mandy's life:

· List of authors to stay inspired by:

1. Dani Johnson
2. Joyce Meyers
3. John Maxwell
4. Nick Vujicic

- List of Mandy's Mentors that have helped her develop skills in Debt & Financial Freedom, Personal Growth, Business Building, and Spiritual Growth:
    1. Dani Johnson - www.danijohnson.com
    2. Dr. LaVonne and Dr. Jack Atnip - http://tecinc.net
    3. Sandi Krakowski - www.arealchange.com/blog
    4. Kathrine Lee - www.ilivethesource.com
    5. Chalene Johnson - www.chalenejohnson.com

CHAPTER 8 – OWN YOUR DESTINY

- Start keeping a sprout journal and write down 3 sprouts every day.
- Begin embracing your destiny and walk proudly in it!

CHAPTER 9 – A LITTLE BIT EVERY DAY

- What one thing can you start today and consistently implement to help you move closer to true wholeness?

CHAPTER 10 – TAKE A DEEP BREATH!

- Give yourself a grace day once a week and enjoy your favorite treat, a favorite TV show, or a favorite activity. Enjoy the journey and take a deep breath!

THE STORY OF YOU

- Take a few moments to stop by and share your story at mandybanderson.com.

END

NOTES

CHAPTER 1 - QUOTE:

http://www.brainyquote.com/quotes/keywords/courage.html

CHAPTER 2 - SCRIPTURE VERSES:

HOLY BIBLE, NEW INTERNATIONAL VERSION ® .
Copyright ©1973, 1978, 1984 by International Bible Society. Used by permission of Zondervan. All rights reserved.

CHAPTER 3 - QUOTE:

http://www.brainyquote.com/quotes/quotes/d/desiderius148997.html

http://dictionary.reference.com/browse/health

CHAPTER 4 – QUOTE:

http://www.brainyquote.com/quotes/topics/topic_forgiveness3.html

CHAPTER 5 - QUOTE:

http://www.brainyquote.com/quotes/authors/h/henry_david_thoreau_11.html

CHAPTER 5 - SCRIPTURE VERSES:

HOLY BIBLE, NEW INTERNATIONAL VERSION ® .
Copyright ©1973, 1978, 1984 by International Bible Society. Used by permission of Zondervan. All rights reserved.

CHAPTER 6 - QUOTE:

http://www.affirmations-for-success.com/free-inspirational-quotes.html

CHAPTER 7 - QUOTE:

http://loveandliterature.tumblr.com/post/8296886402/there-are-people-who-take-the-heart-out-of-you

CHAPTER 8 - QUOTE:

on the Oprah Facebook Page
https://www.facebook.com/oprahwinfrey?ref=ts posted on Wednesday, September 7, 2011

CHAPTER 9 - QUOTE:

http://www.goodreads.com/author/quotes/838305.Mother_Teresa

CHAPTER 10 - QUOTE:

http://lovelavishly.com/post/8984452379/hurdles

CONCLUSION - QUOTE:

http://www.inspirational-quotations.com/wisdom-quotes.html

YOUR NEXT STEP - QUOTE:

http://www.inspirational-quotations.com/wisdom-quotes.html

MANDY B. ANDERSON

WANTS TO HEAR FROM YOU

FOR MORE INFORMATION

For more information on Mandy B. Anderson products, or to find out how to book Mandy for your next event, contact:

MandyBAnderson.com
547 South 7th Street
Box 174
Bismarck, ND 58504

www.MandyBAnderson.com

Made in the USA
San Bernardino, CA
29 May 2013